Heartfelt Praise

Tragic Magic is filled with the kind of beauty and richness common in great literary works of fiction. But Regan Caruthers' story is true, authentic, raw, and filled with the hard-won inspiration of a life dedicated to discovering the truth of who she is. A radiant expressive powerful soul is she, carrying a sword of truth and love for a humanity struggling to find its way back to love or at least, community. Regan's story is both aspirational and invitational. Her entire life she aspired to be all that she was designed to be and she never wavered from that inner commitment, even when outer circumstances required her to go "underground" for survival. At the same time her story invites us to be so truthful with our own struggles, our own boundaries, our own suffering, and our own sense of care for self and others. Everyone can gain something life-changing from this powerful memoir. I have.

—Bruce Cryer, Founder Renaissance Human, Former CEO and Co-creator HeartMath Institute

Tragic Magic by Regan Caruthers shines with the vitality of a fully lived life. With raw honesty and a fearless heart, Caruthers invites readers to walk beside her, sharing her journey from a turbulent childhood to a spiritual awakening that reshapes her entire worldview. Along the way, she weaves stories of triumph in business and the painful challenges of family, leading to a near-death experience that offers a profound reflection on the sacredness of life. Full of soul and resilience, Tragic Magic is not just a memoir—it's a spiritual journey that calls you to live with deeper grace, purpose, and unshakable love for the magic found in even the hardest moments.

—Brad Wetzler, author of Into the Soul of the World: My Journey to Healing

Tragic Magic is the timeless story of a woman finding her power through her relationship with the divine and yet it is so much more. Regan shares with readers the very real struggle of growing up in the shadows of family secrets and dysfunction as well as brilliance and devotion. Through her mother's gift of deep love, her father's gift of wit, and her own gift of spiritual intuition, Regan has gifted us a story of compassion and forgiveness that the world can use as a template for our own healing.

—Nicole Sallak Anderson, novelist and author of Wildfire: Losing Everything, Gaining the World

It's astonishing to me that I'm writing a testimonial for Regan. As a Jewish woman from New York with a background in marketing, our lived experiences have almost nothing in common. I first met Regan over a year ago to help build her brand. What I wasn't prepared for was the powerful story she had to share. I devoured Tragic Magic, eagerly anticipating each new chapter. Regan is a master storyteller, able to convey emotion and vulnerability with such vividness that it left me simultaneously exhausted and exhilarated. Even my cynical self was captivated, and I was disappointed when the book ended; I'm looking forward to a sequel. Regan's raw and emotional account of her struggles, her victories, and the spirit guides that ultimately saved her life offered me a glimpse into something far more significant. It's a sense of hope—something intangible yet tangible, a realization that with effort, something extraordinary is within reach. Read Tragic Magic—if not for the journey, then for the destination.

—Lisa Hermann, Brand Strategist

TRAGIC MAGIC

TRAGIC MAGIC

A MEMOIR

REGAN CARUTHERS

TiPS PUBLISHING SERVICES

Copyright © 2025 Regan Caruthers

All rights reserved. No portion of this book may be reproduced or transmitted in any form by any means, electronic, mechanical, photocopying, recording, or otherwise, without permission in writing from the copyright holder. For information on obtaining permission for reprints or excerpts, contact Regan Caruthers at regancaruthers.com.

Front cover illustration: Lisa Hermann.
Cover and interior design: Robert Kern, TIPS Publishing Services

Library of Congress Control Number: 202491124

print ISBN: 978-1-890586-84-3
ebook ISBN: 978-1-890586-85-0

28 27 26 25   1 2 3 4

To my mother.
My first and most impactful teacher.
Je t'aime infiniment.

Contents

Introduction vii

Chapter 1. Blocked 1
Chapter 2. Layered Grief 7
Chapter 3. Unbridled Power 17
Chapter 4. Foundation 25
Chapter 5. Polarity...................................... 35
Chapter 6. Achieve 41
Chapter 7. Freedom Through Work 49
Chapter 8. Awakening.................................. 55
Chapter 9. Trauma...................................... 67
Chapter 10. Love and Marriage 75
Chapter 11. Heading West 83
Chapter 12. Goodbye 99
Chapter 13. Adapt 105
Chapter 14. Rise and Fall 113
Chapter 15. Endings 123
Chapter 16. On My Own 131
Chapter 17. A Bridge.................................. 135
Chapter 18. A True New Beginning 139
Chapter 19. Transitions............................... 147
Chapter 20. Surrender................................ 153

Chapter 21. Broken Open.............................. 161
Chapter 22. Returning................................ 167
Chapter 23. Madness................................. 171
Chapter 24. Heeding the Call......................... 179
Chapter 25. Broken Heart............................ 189
Chapter 26. Miracle.................................. 205
Chapter 27. Inflamed................................. 211
Chapter 28. In Service............................... 217

Epilogue... 221
Acknowledgments 225

Introduction

For most of my life, I was a woman of two worlds. I was a corporate executive in Silicon Valley, thriving in the fast-paced, high-stakes environment that rewarded ambition and logic. Yet beneath my charismatic veneer, a deeper, more ancient current ran through me—an intuitive knowing, a connection to something greater, a voice that whispered of another way.

This other way was introduced to me in grade school, where my days included meditation, Tai Chi for gym, and songs celebrating Divine love, prayer, and conscious thought. But I buried these teachings as I sought social acceptance during my teenage years, craving safe spaces away from the violence and chaos of my childhood home.

My story is one of hope, marked by intense contrast. The trauma of my youth left deep imprints, and much of my life was spent searching for an escape. My inherited psychic sensitivity overwhelmed me, and I struggled to make sense of it all. I sought normalcy, believing that achievement would bring safety—but it didn't.

A dramatic spiritual awakening in my late 20s shifted my priorities and path, but even then, I continued to struggle with unhealed traumas. It wasn't until I returned to the wisdom teachings of my early life and committed to a disciplined spiritual practice that my life began to transform. I learned to embrace the darkness within me and the darkness reflected in our collective experience. By bringing Divine love to this darkness, I found liberation.

My journey was neither linear nor easy, marked by pain, loss, and the consequences of neglecting spiritual discipline. As I healed childhood wounds and recommitted to the spiritual practices of my youth, I discovered a profound and pure love that transcended human understanding. This love came not from another person but from within—a Divine source that had always been there, waiting for me to remember. It was the love of the Divine, a love that saved my life and transformed me from the inside out.

Tragic Magic is not just my story; it is the story of anyone who has faced their shadows and emerged reborn. It is a testament to the power of faith, the resilience of the human spirit, and the miraculous ways the Divine intervenes when we surrender and commit.

As you read these pages, my hope is that you find reflections of your own journey in mine. May you draw courage from my vulnerability, strength from my surrender, and inspiration from the realization that love is the most powerful force available to us. This is my story—one of tragedy, yes, but also of magic, of a life redeemed and a heart reborn in the crucible of Divine love.

Welcome. All of you are welcome.

Chapter 1. **Blocked**

Exhausted and drained of anything that felt like me, I gathered the little energy I had and threw on a navy cashmere sweater, which was too warm for the heat. I had packed clothes better suited for my home in Santa Cruz than the quaint town of Nevada City, where I had traveled to that morning with the intention to renew. And write.

I had no idea where I would walk, yet I sensed that if I left my Airbnb's opulent safety, I would find something to shift me out of the depression consuming me.

This feeling had come on suddenly, only an hour or so into my trip. Alone, without the distraction of tending to my home or family, with only the interstate hum and the stunning Sierra landscape, I could finally feel what was present within me. While I had a devoted second husband, healthy children, and a stable home, I felt gripped with emotional heaviness. I was at a complete loss because nothing in my day-to-day experience could account for what was happening. Life right now finally had ease, yet I felt heavy, sad, and hopeless.

I ventured out to the streets of Nevada City seeking a solution, but had to stop every few minutes to rest. This simple walk felt like unapproachable exertion. My body felt heavy, like I was carrying a physical weight. I judged myself as I walked. *How the hell am I going to write feeling this way? Why do I feel so inept, so unable to shift?* I knew I needed to free myself from it—somehow—if I was going to write.

My intention on this trip was to begin to write a book—*this* book. To tell a story intended to bring healing to readers—and myself—by sharing my journey of how a turbulent life ultimately was alchemized into a transformation, born first from grace, and then sustained by conscious, deliberate action. I had learned that healing from trauma was infinitely layered. Like a spiral, I had learned how to continually return to the trauma within, bringing new awareness, new processes to the traumatic memories held within my tissues to finally master the process of inner alchemy. Having learned how to tend and heal the trauma within me, I wanted nothing more than to begin to write about what I learned to be in service to others, for I knew that one thing we all share is trauma of one kind or another, corrupted by its influence as it colors how we see the world and ourselves. Yet in that moment, this dream felt impossible.

I walked both aimlessly and purposefully, forcing myself to continue, and trying to sense guidance. I looked in the windows of the shops that adorned Broad Street, appreciating the diversity of merchants in this small town who were mostly ignoring the pandemic and living life. Bars were filled with unmasked customers, live music blared into the streets, people gathered as if there was no pandemic. The aliveness of my surroundings contrasted sharply with the deadness that consumed me. And as I continued walking, I sensed I was close to a destination drawing me near.

Then I saw it: a bohemian gift shop, next to an ice cream parlor with toddlers trying to keep the ice cream balanced on their cones, pink dripping down the face of a boy who struggled to walk securely while managing the melting cone in the afternoon sun. A chalkboard sign read "Tarot Reading." I put my mask on out of courtesy to the shop owner and the customers browsing the pendulums, Mary paintings, Buddha statues, and handmade jewelry filling the shelves. "How much does a tarot reading cost?" I asked the woman behind the counter. As I asked, I felt a bit self-conscious. *How silly that that was my first question.* Access to money was not my issue, and frankly, I would have paid thousands of dollars if it had relieved me from the weight of my grief.

I was told there was a wait, so I ventured out of the store to smoke and ground myself. Organic American Spirits were often my choice to do this. Just as Native Americans use tobacco to carry prayers to the unseen world, I intended to use tobacco in a sacred way as I waited. My deepest moment of connection with another human being centered on smoking with my mother, so I found my occasional smoking a blessing. I made sure I was not near anyone and then breathed in the smoke deeply, prayerfully. Then I re-entered the store after spraying myself with organic lavender hand sanitizer, aware of the irony. Tucked away in the corner of the store was a woman, in her fifties, like me, I guessed, with a silk shawl draped over her shoulders, candles burning on top of the small table that housed her cards, sage, and incense. I sat and told her my name and birthdate, and she asked me to focus on my questions before handing me the tarot deck.

Why do I feel so stuck? What is this overwhelming, consuming feeling of grief, depression, lack of aliveness? I asked these questions silently as I shuffled the deck. I asked my guides to come forth and support me in gaining revelation.

The tarot reader asked me to divide the deck into three smaller decks and place them on the table. She explained that the first cards she would draw were reflections of me, my essence, my fundamental strengths. She confidently pulled the first card: The Empress. She explained that earthly manifestation comes easily to me, that this card reflects creativity, abundance, and connection to the Earth and new life in all its forms. Two words best describe this card: creative intelligence. Then Justice, reflecting balance, the moral order of things, and The Sun, symbolizing vitality and success. Then the Queen of Cups, representing psychic ability, the Six of Wands, representing achievement and success. Then, finally, she pulled the King of Cups, representing mastery over the unconscious.

I felt validated as she shared these cards: I could see how they aligned with my strengths. I had indeed experienced professional success. Through personal study, I had learned how to balance myself and find emotional sovereignty when met with chaotic circumstances. And I had known since childhood that I was psychic. And all of this was reflected in the cards.

But the last card, the King of Cups, *mastery over the unconscious*, compelled the most reflection. I had spent many years deliberately bringing focused attention to my unconscious beliefs, traumas, and actions. I wanted to bring these forces to conscious awareness because I knew I couldn't heal what I didn't acknowledge. In that spirit, my purpose in sitting with the tarot reader was to bring to awareness the origin of the depressive weight I was carrying.

Then she explained that the next cards would be focused on what was in my way. First she drew the Five of Cups, symbolizing sorrow over past events. She then pulled the Ten of Swords, symbolizing exhaustion, betrayal, and victimization. I began to cry as I gazed at this mix of cards and their precise reflection of what was alive and dead inside me. The cards were acting like a trusted friend, reflecting the truth as they saw it.

As the tears flowed, I felt a release. I had known all of it—exhaustion, betrayal, and victimization. I thought I had processed throughout my life what was mine, but now feelings of deep grief continued to rise to the surface. I had tried to force myself to cry many times that day on my journey to Nevada City, yet it was as if the grief had found residence inside of me and wouldn't be evicted. Finally, now, I could weep, the conversation deepened, and the revelation emerged, along with the question: *were some of these feelings not mine?*

Since continuing to pay for the tarot reader's time was not an issue, I began to tell her explicitly what led me to her. I sensed she had access to an intuitive intelligence that could help me. "I've come here to write my story. I feel so stuck and heavy with an all-consuming depressive grief. If you have time, I'd like to share more."

I began to tell her about when it had all begun, ten years before.

Chapter 2. **Layered Grief**

On the unkempt lawn of my soon-to-be ex-husband Michael's home, the home we shared briefly before separating, I wept.

I was there to talk to the man who I had left, yet still held a deep love for, who I still relied on for connection and support. Our separation was new. I had moved out only a few months before this visit and my new home was a bike ride away. Thankfully, I had found a beautiful home to rent nearby, with a spectacular view of the ocean. I wanted our teenage sons to feel like they could move freely between both houses with little separating us. And while there was little physical distance between us, I felt so alone. I was an only child with two dead parents, choosing to leave my husband, breaking up the nuclear family I had helped create, because the emotional and financial instability inherent in the marriage was more than I could bear.

I couldn't hold it in any longer. I let the tears out. As I grieved and Michael listened, I appreciated that our friendship had endured. I was clear about what I was suffering, knew its dimensions: I was grieving the breakup of my family. The loss of the family I chose to leave and the sudden loss of my mother, who had died a few months before I moved out of the home I had shared with Michael. And I was grieving the estrangement that came as an only child who knew so little about my father's family. My father had died over a decade before and I had no one I trusted to ask about them. My questions about that side of the family had no resolution, no way of knowing who they were, what their lives were like. My past was like trying to finish a jigsaw puzzle, but with the final pieces missing. Lost. I felt there were crucial parts of myself that I could only understand by knowing more about them.

As I wept under the hot sun in Michael's yard, memories of my mother's shocking death a few months earlier flooded my mind.

Before moving out, I had hosted a birthday party to celebrate Michael's fiftieth birthday. Even though I was divorcing him, and our family and friends knew our marriage was ending, I wanted to celebrate his life. I wanted to ensure that our children, friends, and family knew our pending divorce didn't mean our love for each other had ended, rather it had changed. As I rushed about the house, cleaning the guest bathroom, knowing I only had a couple of hours to get everything ready for the party, the phone rang. The ring felt ominous. I answered, a cleaning rag still in hand as my stepfather explained that he had gone to wake my mother from a nap and found her dead. I felt empty, numb, shocked, and alone. My mother had always said that she would die taking a nap. Once again, her intuition was accurate.

Now collapsed with grief on the stoop of my ex's home, I felt into all the layers of loss. I knew in time I would fully grieve the loss of my mother and husband. Yet how would I reconcile my unknown ancestry? My father had always acted as if our common ancestry shouldn't be spoken about. I deeply regretted not asking more questions when he was alive. All this swelled within me as I continued to cry and name what was within.

"You know, Regan, you have grieved about knowing so little about your family for many years. It would help if you did something about it." Michael seemed to be growing impatient and losing his capacity for empathy.

"Well, I have no idea what to do. The only thing to do, I guess, is to pray." So I stood, tears blurring my vision, as I loudly articulated a prayer to my paternal ancestors, there in front of Michael. "I just want to know you and, in so knowing, have insight into myself." I prayed with clarity.

I said a tearful goodbye to Michael and returned to my seaside rental. Adorning the walls of my beach house were beautifully framed photographs of ancestors whose names I didn't know, whose stories were never told to me. Before moving to California some twenty years ago, I had found a box of old photographs in my mother's basement and made a heartfelt decision not to leave the photos in the frayed box that housed them with patches of mold splattered about, as if it was some Rorschach test, and spent thousands of dollars to frame each one. I wanted to show respect to those who came before.

As I showered off the grief back at home, I closed my eyes, comforted by the cleansing, hot water. I had stared at their photographs so many times before; their faces were etched in my mind as I closed my eyes in the shower and kept my prayer alive in my awareness. The phone rang as I stepped out of the shower, but I let it go to voicemail, curious about who was calling; my landline hardly rang anymore. Now dressed, I checked my voicemail.

It was a woman with a heavy Dutch accent. Marion Hubscher, she introduced herself, explained in her message that her grandmother was my paternal great-grandmother's sister. She ended her message saying, "I hope you call me back. I just want to know you and, in so knowing, have insight into myself."

I was stunned.

Having prayed just twenty minutes before to my paternal ancestors, her precise reflection back of my prayer amazed me with the magnitude of what was happening. This phone call, this new connection with a distant relative I didn't know I had, had just launched me into a journey of learning about the ancestral trauma that had been held secret for generations.

Although I spoke with Marion on the phone a number of times, it would be seven years before I was able to travel to Amsterdam to meet her in person.

"Before I share this with you, I need your explicit permission." Marion had empathetic reservation as I sat at her kitchen table in her modest flat. I had traveled to Amsterdam to visit her, and she was going to share with me all she had learned about our common ancestry. We saw several modest homes in The Hague, where my paternal lineage had lived before immigrating to New York City in the early 1900s. I took countless photos, including of the cigar shop my great-grandfather owned, which was an architecturally stunning example of his consistently failed business enterprises. It seemed like the perfect symbol of the pressure that preceded their immigration; extravagance without the legitimate means to support it was a thread I sensed ran through this part of my family.

"Of course, Marion, I want to know everything you have learned."

With my permission now in place, she placed a newspaper on the table. I read the salacious headline that covered the front page, "AMAZING AFTERMATH OF KANSAS CITY'S FAMOUS TRIANGLE PLOT." I recognized my grandmother immediately. Her movie-star good looks were hard to forget. I also saw a picture of my forlorn father, just two years old, sitting next to a large dog, which I assumed was the family pet. Two other men I didn't recognize were also pictured: a stately man who looked very much like my father and a local grocer. The story revealed a series of events that read like a bizarre made-for-television movie plot.

In 1925, claiming she feared for her life, Abby Vieweg, my grandmother, had hired her local grocer, who delivered her groceries to her well-appointed home, giving him $600 to find and hire a hitman on her behalf. Six hundred dollars was a significant amount of money for that time—approximately $10,000 in today's dollars. She wanted her Russian husband, my grandfather, dead, claiming that he was running a crime syndicate and she feared for her life. Kansas City in 1925 was a hotbed for organized crime at the height of prohibition. When the naïve and romantically smitten grocer hired the hitman, he didn't realize that the man he hired was an undercover detective for the police. The police chose to let the planned hit play out further and then arrested my grandmother and the grocer for conspiracy to commit murder. The Missouri Supreme Court decided the case after many years, on appeal, where they ruled to acquit my grandmother on a statutory technicality.

Empathy flooded my system as I sat at Marion's table and read the many newspaper articles she had collected about this strange series of events. I thought about my father as a little boy on the run with a private nurse his father had hired the week of his mother's arrest. Journalists across the country reported about how my father was with this nurse—a stranger to him—as my grandfather tried to keep the courts from assigning his son to the state's care. After my grandmother's acquittal, my grandparents briefly reconciled out of love for their young son. Yet the reconciliation was brief, divorce followed, and my grandfather was awarded custody of my father. He enrolled my now five-year-old father in military school in Illinois, clearly not thinking of what was in my Dad's best interest—or perhaps the choice was an act of great love, for what did a gangster know about raising a son?

I learned a lot from Marion during our visit, but there was still more to discover.

**

A few weeks before my trip to Nevada City to launch my writing project, I received a report that I had commissioned from a group of professional genealogists. I learned about them from my favorite PBS show, *Finding Your Roots*. If the host and Harvard professor, Henry Louis Gates, relied on these researchers to learn about the ancestral past of the celebrities who came on his show, then I knew they could help me learn more details of my father's ordeal.

When the package arrived, I had to steady myself; I had an intense mix of emotions. Excitement, dread, and anticipation stirred within me as I opened the box to reveal a spiral bound report three inches thick.

My questions to them were: where was Dad while his mother's crime was being adjudicated? Did my grandfather really run a crime syndicate, as my grandmother had claimed? And where did the name Caruthers come from?

I learned that after my grandfather's sudden death of a heart attack at the Fox Theater in St. Louis in 1930 when my father was seven, my grandmother was awarded custody. She traveled to pick him up from military school with her newest love interest, a man named Ray Caruthers. I remembered just a few conversations that my Dad and I had about his young life, though it was clear to me now that he had kept hidden the truth of what he had endured out of shame and trauma. I recalled his edited version of that time in his life, sharing that when his mother picked him up, she said coldly, "Your father is dead. Meet your new father." His new "father," Ray Caruthers, was in my father's life for less than a year.

My name, Regan Caruthers, had suddenly taken on new meaning. I had always felt great pride in the reputation of my family name, given my father's influence in my hometown of St. Louis, where had been the most revered litigator in generations. Now, I felt differently knowing the truth. The name reflected deceit. Another ancestral choice shrouded in trauma and secrecy. My father chose the name Caruthers when he registered for Social Security in 1935, after FDR introduced this new program to provide greater economic security to the masses during the Great Depression. And while my father was just twelve years old, everyone was encouraged to register. Back then, you could name yourself whatever you chose. There were no databases or computers, and given how many immigrants changed their names once arriving at Ellis Island, it was a common practice. My guess was he wanted to distance himself from the front-page news that had adorned the dailies across the country for years following my grandmother's arrest. The "triangle plot" was the talk of towns coast to coast. And so my father, born Rexford Frank, became Rexford Caruthers.

I learned too that the name Frank was yet another deception. My grandfather had hidden his identity by changing his last name from Lourie to Frank. My grandparents had met in New York City. Their clandestine affair broke hearts, for my grandfather left a wife and three young children for my grandmother. The lovers took off together and conceived my father, born as they traveled in Louisville, Kentucky, before settling in Kansas City.

Despite all of this, my father was awarded a full ride to Harvard less than a decade after being picked up by his mother at military school. Too poor to afford even the travel to Boston, he chose to begin his undergraduate education instead at Washington University in St. Louis, where he, his mother, and her parents had settled after the Kansas City drama had come to an end. When my father, Rexford Caruthers—or was it Rexford Frank, or Rexford Lourie?—died in 2001, he was described in his obituary as the greatest legal mind to ever practice law in St. Louis.

***

As I sat with the tarot reader, telling her this tale, I began to realize what was going on for me.

It may seem far-fetched that anyone could be affected emotionally by the choices of people long dead, yet research into intergenerational trauma demonstrates that trauma gets passed down both socially through interactions with a family whose trauma remains unresolved, and genetically, since we inherit the traumatized genes of our ancestors. A simple Google search of "intergenerational trauma" will yield hundreds of results—studies by the National Institutes of Health, the American Psychological Association, and many more, as our culture has finally begun to document how trauma is passed down from one generation to the next.

The trauma that my father experienced in the 1920s was alive in me in 2021. I was still holding my father's and his parents' unresolved grief. I'd seen deep trauma almost jumping off the page of the report—what Dad had endured as a young boy, the shame and regret his parents, my grandparents, felt about their choices. They were all somehow affecting me here and now. Finally, I could sense that this was the source of the overwhelming emotional weight I'd been dragging along with me on this trip.

The tarot reader affirmed that I was holding the unprocessed grief of my ancestors. She counseled me to create a ceremony to allow myself to feel it deeply and to call upon these ancestors so that we could cry together, honor our collective pain, and conclude by affirming unconditional love and forgiveness for each other and ourselves. Her counsel felt deeply resonant.

As I exited the store, it was now after 6:00 p.m. on a Sunday in a small town—most stores were closed. Where could I find some candles to use in the ceremony I was to create that night? My newfound clarity has roused a sense of urgency in me. I also needed to buy some cold brew for the morning, and I remembered a convenience store on Broad Street near my Airbnb. I said a quick prayer about finding candles and entered. I asked the cashier if they had candles, and in a heavy Indian accent, he said, "Yes, below the batteries." And there were the candles, each adorned with the faces of archangels and my greatest teacher, Jesus. So I picked two—Jesus and the archangel Michael—thinking I needed their strength to heal the grief I was carrying for my family.

As I walked home with the heavy weight of my grief, my coffee, and my candles, the radiant full moon beamed above me. I sensed a feeling of hope for the first time in a long time. I entered my Airbnb, immediately undressed, lit the candles, and filled my bathtub.

Night had fallen and the moon shone brightly through the window above the tub. I centered myself by first connecting to my heart. I took deep breaths as I focused on the area of my heart, directing my focus to the inhales and exhales, bringing my hand over my heart to help me focus. Once I fell into an easeful rhythm of breathing, I recalled a moment when I felt deeply loved by my father. I remembered his loving embrace as I lay in his hospice bed, wondering if his next breath would be his last. His love for me at that moment held no ego. It felt very similar to holding a newborn in your arms. I focused on re-experiencing that moment of expansive, nurturing, unconditional love. I soaked in the feeling, and as I did, I felt peace and receptivity growing within me. I then began calling in my ancestors, my father, his mother and father, their mother and father, and any other ancestor who wanted to be present. I asked them to gather with me, and I visualized us all holding hands to form a circle. I don't recall exactly what I said, but I know I cried deeply. I asked them to honor our collective grief, shame, and trauma together with me. I affirmed my unconditional love for them. I reminded them that the purpose of coming to Earth was to learn and evolve. I reminded them that they had all done that. I asked them to join me in affirming that coming here had fulfilled our purpose. I affirmed with them that it was all okay. Ultimately, who we are beneath the unaligned choices, the conflict, and the pain we create and subject ourselves to is love, for it is what we are made of. I closed by saying, out loud in my darkening room, "I love you. I forgive you. I am grateful for your choices; they have informed my path and created me." Then I exclaimed, "I am fantastic. I am an agent of love and transformation in part because of you. Thank you!"

I drained the tub and blew out the candles, feeling profoundly alive and cleansed. An hour or so later, I fell into my first restful sleep in months. And when I awakened, after a modest breakfast, I finally began to write.

Chapter 3. Unbridled Power

Seeking a tarot reader's counsel was perhaps not a typical or conventional choice. Yet, seeking spiritual solutions to life's ever-present challenges had become second nature for me. My mother's uncanny intuitive sight and non-conventional ways of spending her time were deeply rooted in my upbringing.

When I was a young girl, my mother would often bring out a deck of cards, each with a different color, and ask me or young friends I had over for sleepovers to choose the cards in order of preference—the cards you liked the most to the least. From that sequence of choices, my mother would interpret your personality, your soul's mission on the Earth, your innate obstacles, and insight into your path forward. My friends never seemed awkward or uncomfortable in her presence; you felt seen and loved, as if you were the most important person in the world to her. When she met strangers, she would often guess their birthdays after a brief hello. She had an undeniable wisdom about her, and in her presence, with few exceptions, you never felt judged, only loved. As a teenager, when my stepfather was out of town fishing, I would gather my friends together for parties loosely supervised by my mother. Within an hour or so there would be a line at least twenty friends deep, single file down the small hallway that led to my mother's bedroom. One at a time my mother would offer her wisdom, her magnanimous love, her insights, and her encouragement to live authentically, take risks, and love without constraint. As a young adult if I ran into old friends from childhood, literally the first question out of their mouths was "How's your Mom?" She had an immediate impact on others. If you knew her, you knew that she was not a typical human in any sense of the word. She was different.

Her innate wisdom and presence stood in sharp contrast to her self-diagnosis in 1961 of manic depression. My father had tricked her into going with him to Renard Mental Hospital, where, surrounded by psychiatrists, she broke through their confusion and named her illness. "You can't agree on a diagnosis now, can you? I'm a manic depressive." She had arrived at Renard in a Bill Blass gray suit, perfectly tailored, with a long strand of pearls that she always knotted, placed consciously on her neckline. After being admitted, they forced her to wear their institutional clothing, after which the male patients gathered around her in curiosity; gorgeous redheads who looked like movie stars were not who they were used to seeing there. My mother often retold the events of this day to me, and the part that she always emphasized was that after her evaluation, she noticed that the other patients had gone outside to play basketball. Eager for their acceptance and connection, she joined them on the court.

"You know, Regan, every time they gave me the ball and I threw it, it went right into the hoop. Now why do you think that is?" She wasn't glib in her question to me; she didn't understand how her sudden mastery of basketball was just an extension of her capacity to connect with all things with grace and power. I have always credited the naming of her illness to my mother's clairvoyance. I believe she pulled this insight out of the air, as I had witnessed countless times her capacity for clarity and wisdom that felt otherworldly. She wasn't a medical scholar; she just *knew*. And this way of knowing is her legacy to me.

Chapter 3. Unbridled Power

With the gift of clairvoyance comes the inherent challenge. Being highly sensitive, as a young girl I could "hear" what others were thinking. Having access to another's inner dialogue overwhelmed me. In the light of day, I felt powerful, capable, and strong. But at night, spirits and shadowy figures filled my room, and visitations by forces that felt and looked like demons were common occurrences haunting me.

I vividly remember the day I finally asked these demonic forces to stop.

Mother had partnered with an unstable and violent man that she had met in the mental hospital a year or so after she and my Dad split up. I would often escape the turmoil in the house by going downstairs to the tiny basement with a tumbling mat as my companion. I would stretch and tumble on it while playing uplifting, light-hearted Broadway show tunes on the turntable, the volume high enough to drown out the chaos and shouting in the rooms above. This allowed me to escape into movement and song.

One day as I was dancing and tumbling in the basement, there he was. Sitting above the washing machine on a fiery throne. He was a frequent visitor. I knew not what he wanted or needed. Terrified, I ran up the steps screaming out loud for it all to stop! As if by my command, my extrasensory perceptions ended abruptly that morning.

I lived the rest of my childhood and young adult life without this extra load on my system. It wouldn't be until the age of twenty-seven that these gifts would come back as abruptly as they had departed, when this same visitor returned to my bedside and changed my life.

Like my father's childhood, my mother's was also trauma filled. She spoke openly with me about it all: the sexual abuse at the hands of her uncles who shared their rat-infested, dilapidated home during the Great Depression; the shame-filled death of her father from syphilis when she was five; her incestuous relationship with her brother; and the abject poverty they endured.

I'm sure that all of it imprinted deeply on my highly sensitive mother, yet she somehow found a way to thrive as a young girl and young adult. She was often the subject of local news, detailing her many achievements in her small industrial town of Fulton, New York. At the age of sixteen, in 1949, she was chosen by the Red Cross to travel to post-war Europe to befriend other Red Cross organizations in Finland, Denmark, and France, and to speak publicly to them about the hope of the post-war era. She received a scholarship to Northwestern, where she became a campus leader and was sponsored again by the Danish government her senior year to continue her work extending friendships to peers there. She enrolled at the Sorbonne in Paris for her postgraduate work in French. She celebrated her career as a flight attendant for Pan Am, where she flew the dignitary flights for President Eisenhower and helped to create the first foreign language laboratory of any major corporation. She was often interviewed by the BBC. Her affair with King Hussein of Jordan is detailed in five letters I have saved in my bureau. Each time I read them, I marvel at the King's impeccable handwriting and the genuine care and affection they felt for each other. And yet her fame, celebrity, and outstanding achievements were not enough to sustain her. Her first husband abused her. She carried a stillborn to term and miscarried many others. Her abusive first marriage was essential in creating me, for to get out of her toxic union, she hired the best legal counsel St. Louis had to offer to represent her in her divorce: my father, Rex Caruthers. They fell deeply in love and conceived me six years later.

I am clear that her manic depression was partly a response to the many traumas that remained untended within her. However, unlike my father, she spoke openly about it all, which at least provided some healing through honest acknowledgment. She held few secrets, and her open heart was both her savior and her curse in that she couldn't regulate the primordial energy that ran through her, ultimately ravaging her to such a degree that from age fifty until her death at seventy-eight, she rarely left the house. Most of her adult life mirrored her childhood—it was rife with instability and poverty after her divorce from my father. Growing up with her was tragic magic. I would often respond "no" when she asked me to go with her in the basement to her trunk where she housed all the newspaper articles, letters from famous people, and artifacts from her early life. I couldn't reconcile the life she had once led with the life I was experiencing with her. The contrast was too painful. It wasn't until I traveled back home for her funeral that I opened the trunk and spent more than a week organizing and reading her history housed there.

Given the exceptional achievements both my parents experienced, you might assume that their lives would continue their meteoric rise, creating wealth, a sense of fulfillment, and stability. But that wasn't so. What I learned witnessing them was akin to being rooted in unstable soil without adequate nutrients but with blasts of sunshine so bright, unbridled in its power.

The constant love from my mother was significant, however, and supported me in sustaining an accessible, deep, and ever-present relationship with the Divine. Yet, as a child I was not conscious of this. I was not taught how to alchemize it all within myself, how to root down and grow up. In time, I had to learn how to access the proper spiritual nutrition I needed to sustain a life. And I had to learn how to live without the grace of models, for I knew I didn't want to emulate what I had witnessed. I would learn in time that prayer and deep surrender to Divine forces could create miracles.

Imagine if we all walked about with poster boards affixed to our bodies, front and back, listing our significant traumas like a grocery list. Would we be kinder to each other? Would we lend a hand more readily if we knew—in simple terms—what others had endured? When I learned more about my family and the destructive choices many of them had made, I could easily see my parents' and my ancestors' humanity more clearly. When we judge people based solely on their behavior, we aren't seeing the trauma underlying each destructive choice. If we did, our judgment would fade, and we would offer compassion and forgiveness more easily.

When I prayed that day as I cried on my ex-husband's front stoop, I declared to my ancestors, *I just want to know you and, in so knowing, have insight into myself.* I believed in prayer's power to facilitate what I was asking. And then Marion Hubscher called minutes after, reflecting almost verbatim the prayer I had offered. I learned then, and more and more over the years, the importance of letting the prayer go, releasing it fully, surrendering it entirely, knowing that the supreme energy that we call God can create truly anything. This tool, this way of being, has been essential to my journey of healing generational trauma and of healing myself.

Prayer, perspective, distance, and healing let me not only see my parent's humanity more clearly, it also let me see their magic.

Perhaps their greatness was a trauma response—fueling their desire for excellence as a way of being "okay"—yet that answer feels inadequate to me. Perhaps instead, their brilliance was the Divine working through them. I have yet to learn what their karma was and what kind of lives they led before this one, but what was clear about both of them was this: they both possessed and could create magic and they both didn't know how to regulate or direct with intention the power that ran through them. They seemed powered by a force they didn't understand or think much about. They were charged, and charged ahead, unconsciously making attempts to heal, or solve, their trauma, but not understanding how to do so.

My father exuded a kind, magnetic power, had a photographic memory, and excelled easily; he was brilliant. The public genuinely loved him, and his peers, many of whom came to honor him at his memorial, spoke eloquently about his impact. And while they spoke of his greatness as an attorney, they also talked about his kind generosity and humanity. Yes, his infidelity and his neglect of me hurt our family, yet what I believe, knowing what I know now, is that his life was a triumph. Similar to Mom, he struggled to sustain and channel his power. He was careless in his investment decisions, reckless with his health and his relationships.

Like Dad, God powered my mother's magnetism, her capacity for profound wisdom. Yet while she went to therapy countless times, it did little to help, for the mental health field in the U.S. often pathologizes and misunderstands spiritual power.

There are many accounts from Indigenous shamans who, upon entering a mental institution, find the patients to be healers who couldn't *integrate the call*. Such wise ones view mental illness as a spiritual emergency, wherein people haven't received the assistance they need to incorporate the energy they are connected to. According to Malidoma Patrice Somé, a West African shaman, mental illness signals "the birth of a healer." Thus, mental disorders are spiritual emergencies and need to be regarded as such so that the healer can be assisted in being born. What those in the West view as mental illness, the Dagara people regard as "good news from the other world." The person going through the crisis is a medium for a message the community needs from the spirit realm. Dr. Somé comments: "Mental disorder, and behavioral disorder of all kinds, signal that two incompatible energies have merged into the same field."

I know in my heart that is what happened to my mother. But instead of getting the help she needed, she was drugged, given electric shock therapy, and forced into residential treatment that dimmed her power and connection and never provided any lasting relief. And while I have not yet shared my own similar experiences here, I know that if I had confided in a mental health professional about either what I saw in the basement as a child or some of the dramatic incidents that came later in my adult life,

I too would have been diagnosed with mental illness and given drugs that would have fundamentally changed my life. Thankfully, my understanding of the truth about my mother enabled me to circumvent this tragedy.

As my life unfolded into adulthood, I would come to know that my most important mission was to heal my childhood trauma so that my unhealed past did not color my perceptions of daily life.

Imagine you're a young child in your backyard when a rattlesnake sits erect, his rattle on full alert. You panic and run inside, but there is no adult there to comfort you. The fear is stored inside you, with no one to share it with and no adult to help you process it. Fast forward, you are now an adult watering your backyard. It's dusk, without adequate light, and you trip over a beige garden hose. For a moment, you panic, your heart beats wildly, and your chest tightens. A snake! The amygdala, an ancient part of your brain, constantly scans the sensory environment looking for matches of what you are experiencing with what you have stored. And while its mission is to keep you safe from harm, it is imprecise.

Healing trauma requires us to be courageous, like a warrior wielding love like a sword; like a traveler with love as a trusted friend, accompanying us to all the stuck, dark, and terror-filled places within us so we can love those places and free ourselves from their corrupted influence. We are all broken in some manner or another. And unhealed, we continue to hand down the traumatized genes and behaviors of those who came before.

I was, and have been, determined to break the cycle so my children could thrive without the weight of ancestral trauma on their backs. I did not want my trauma and my traumatized genes to color my perception of reality. When we are triggered, it is a call from our unhealed selves for attention, for healing. And while our physiology is trying to keep us safe by triggering reactions that enable fight and flight, I knew I wanted to be sovereign from my wounding. The only way to experience that was to heal.

Chapter 4. **Foundation**

My mother's intuition directed her to choose an elementary school where honoring my Divine nature, the vital importance of emotional self-regulation, and the transformative power of love were fostered. Although my father wanted me to attend Community School, an elementary school for the St. Louis elite, my mother knew better and enrolled me, at age four, at Forsyth School.

This unique school would foster emotional and spiritual health that would ultimately save my life. And while its profound lessons only became conscious in my late twenties, what I learned there established a foundation I later drew upon—when I was ready.

Forsyth School was founded in 1961 by three women who had befriended each other when studying the philosophy of Charles Fillmore, the founder of the Unity Church. They began this transformative school in the basement of the Unity Church on the corner of Skinker and Forsyth Boulevards in St. Louis. By the time I was enrolled, some ten years after its founding, they had the means to purchase a beautiful, stately home, the first of many schoolhouses Forsyth would acquire in following years.

My mother would often recount the story of my first day in which I insisted that I walk in alone. At age four, my classmates were being walked in by their parents, but I had already decided to rely only on myself.

While I didn't know this on my first day, or for years to come, the founders were *awake*. What I mean is that they all had a profoundly committed and disciplined spiritual life and believed that what children needed more than anything else was love, freedom, and affirmation of their Divine nature.

Each day began with morning assembly. Mary Dunbar, one of the founders, would play the piano as we sang and learned songs that reflected the school's philosophy.

"Look for love, look for love when the dawn light is breaking, look for love. Look for love in the evening when the stars are waking. Look for love, look for love, and when you do. Look for love, and love will be right there looking at you."

"If you believe in a world full of woe, it is done to you as you believe. And if you believe that to learn is to grow, it is done to you, as you believe. It is done to you, as you believe. So I choose to believe in things that are good, for it is done to you, as you believe. If you give thanks for a beautiful day, it is done to you, as you believe. And if you lovingly choose life, it is done to you, as you believe. It is done to you, as you believe. So I choose to believe in things that are good, for it is done to you as you believe."

"Something wonderful, something grand, something wonderful is happening right where I stand. Through my mind and through my body, through all I do and say, good morning, good morning world, oh, isn't it a wonderful day!"

"It's up to you what you are going to do with your life. It's up to you what you're going to be. It's up to you; you've got the power to choose in your life. It's up to you to be free. Are you going to have a good day? Will you live it in peace? You can learn to light your way; just learn to pray without ceasing. You make the world, you know. Your thoughts are key. Every loving thought you show, you'll feel the glow of your being."

Each day, in addition to the morning assembly, we would be guided in meditation, led to visualize what we wanted to accomplish and learn that day. On occasion, we would photograph our energy field with Kirlian film. We practiced Tai Chi led by a Chinese immigrant who had mastery of the practice. We learned Algebra, Latin, and French and read the classics. I remember creating a report on Denmark, at the unlikely age of seven, which I illustrated with various graphs about their demographics, industry, agriculture, and culture. We didn't have grades or grade levels at Forsyth. Instead we were met individually with projects that reflected our interests and strengths. I was fascinated with my mother's stories of living in Copenhagen, so my report reflected and deepened that interest.

We were only tested once a year by Iowa Basic Testing, which I assume was needed for accreditation. This annual test measured student performance on the exam in terms of academic grades. During my last year at the school, I opened the envelope containing my test results. I felt proud and accomplished as I read the results of my reading comprehension: tenth-grade 9th month. At the age of ten, my reading level was as if I was almost a high school junior.

After a few years at Forsyth, when I was seven, I pleaded with my mother to go to the local elementary school instead so I could be with my neighborhood friends. And while I loved projects like my recent report on Denmark, I longed to be with friends who lived nearby. My mother agreed to let me give Riverbend Elementary a try. Given my age, the school chose to put me in the first grade. I was escorted to a large classroom that housed about thirty students and my mother and the principal were in the back of the classroom observing me. As I sat down, excited to be there and eager for recess so I could play with my best friend, Nancy, I was handed a worksheet that had a sizeable, uncolored clown on the front, and at the bottom of the worksheet was a dashed line area to guide my printing where I was to write a sentence about the clown. While I didn't swear then, my internal response was, *What the hell?* I felt demeaned. *You want me to color and write within the lines?* It was, of course, a perfect metaphor for public schooling: stay within the lines. Do what you're told. Sit down. Shut up. I felt unseen and fundamentally disrespected. After asking permission to get a drink of water, my mother motioned to me, gesturing a *Well? How do you like it?* I emphatically gestured a thumbs down as I returned promptly to my seat. I returned the next day to Riverbend because the planned field trip to a local bread factory sounded fun, but those two days were all I had of public school until I returned to public education for middle and high school.

I vividly remember in my last year at Forsyth singing in the play yard over and over again the hit song by Nicolette Larson. *It's going to take a lot of love to change how things are.* That song was my anthem, a foreshadowing, which sometimes gives us clues of what's to come, like any great story does.

Indeed the power of love, the actual energy of love, would ultimately save my life and help transform those around me. But for now, what I learned at Forsyth School, and the love that my mother could radiate, even as she suffered, were the two most influential aspects of my young life.

It wasn't until years later that I realized how innovative and effective a learning environment Forsyth School was. I left it having never experienced homework or testing (except for that Iowa Test, of course). Some life events are so profound that words feel inadequate to describe their impact; that is how I think about my early schooling. Without the teachings there, I can't imagine who I would have become. I was able to cultivate a conscious relationship with the truth of who I actually am: a unique expression of the Divine itself. I learned the vital importance of prayer. Learning through song, through the meditative movement of Tai Chi, by sitting quietly, and visualizing every day what I want to experience and create provided me with the internal capacity to navigate the chaos and trauma of early life. When we truly understand that we are both Divine and eternal, we can better cope with life's complexity. We also then have freedom available within us, which enables us to speak truth and feel empowered because we sense the true power within us.

An aspect of this phenomenon, the power of thought, was documented by Dr. Masaru Emoto, who photographed water molecules at the moment of freezing, showing that the structure of water itself is impacted by what we think and feel. Water that was sent love and offered loving words displayed a frozen structure of beauty and symmetry. In contrast, water that was sent feelings of anger, harsh words and destructive thought had a fractured, broken and disturbed looking molecular structure. And as a young girl at school, I saw in real time how my thoughts and feelings affected the Kirlian photography of my energy field. The more loving and at peace I felt, the more vibrant and clear my energy field was. Informed still by my transformative early education, as I approach my fifty-seventh birthday, I use this prayerful affirmation everyday:

> I open myself to my highest knowing, to my highest expression. I ask for help from my angels, guides, and ancestors to give me the insights, resources, and experiences to experience my highest good and to be an agent of Divine love. I radiate this feeling of love to all the unhealed places within me.

It was at Forsyth that I learned how to cultivate an inner voice, an inner guidance that literally has never failed me.

As a young adult, the founders long retired, I traveled to Florida, pregnant with my first child, to visit with the founder, Mary Dunbar. I asked her if she could choose just one thing, what did she hope the experience of the school taught us as a lasting legacy? She quickly answered, "I wanted you to know that every thought and feeling you have is your choice."

This confirmed for me what I felt I had learned there; the spiritual principles that guided our instruction, as well as direct experiences of my intuitive nature, created an unconscious capacity in me to have more sovereignty in dealing with the craziness of my upbringing.

While I recognize that few people have experienced a formative education as I had, we all still have the opportunity to cultivate, beginning right now, a more intimate relationship with ourselves that will lead us to heal, as we develop greater intimacy with our true natures. A simple daily practice, just as I experienced as a little girl, to sit quietly, focusing your attention on your heart, and recall any moment when you felt love and gratitude—for anything. Once identified, deliberately re-experience that feeling. Bathe in its comfort and expansive intelligence. The heart's voice is quiet and still, and by listening, we are directed to make transformative choices and can experience breakthroughs. While it takes time and daily commitment, you will find, as the saying goes, that your heart will lead the way and will help bring your perception back to your Divine nature. So, I invite you to begin this contact with your heart with a daily commitment to listening to this foundation of your being. When we spend time opening and honoring its innate intelligence, it will begin to heal and lead us. When we cultivate feelings of love and gratitude for anything at all, while intending to sense the generous support that surrounds us, even if we don't yet believe it, we can begin to change the composition of what is stored in our amygdalas.

The funny thing about the brain is that it doesn't distinguish between something we are directly experiencing and its emotional composition with something we recall. Just like you can add something to offset a soup that's too salty, you can add to your amygdala moments filled with feelings of love and gratitude by simply remembering one and re-experiencing the emotions as if they are happening in the now. And the more you do this, the more you change the composition of the emotional memories stored by the amygdala, shifting the ratio to the positive; this in turn shifts your daily perceptions; you become less triggered; and you begin to see the external world differently. As your perceptual system shifts, you'll feel more hope, ease, and less emotional disturbance. And as you connect to feelings of love and gratitude, you can add prayerful affirmations that suit your intention. Words are powerful; just as Dr. Emoto's research demonstrated, each word we utter has an underlying energy.

During that visit with Mary Dunbar, I also learned how connected to Divine intelligence she was. During our visit, she shared a story about the day the school first opened. As she walked down the grand staircase, she was so full of her connection to spirit that she hadn't even planned the day. She was fully surrendered, letting Divine intelligence direct what she said and did with the children. I also learned that in the summers she would take children failing in the inner-city public schools and give them an eight-week program—with no emphasis on reading, writing, or arithmetic. By the end of their time with her, she would have them all performing at grade level.

How? She taught them how to love themselves. She taught them that a guiding force, uniquely intelligent and benevolent, wanted them to thrive and loved them unconditionally. She taught them meditation. Academic work is easy when you know how to quiet your mind while accessing the Divine intelligence within you.

Public school settings today stand in stark contrast. One can't speak of God or Source or Spirit or whatever you choose to call the Divine. One can't explicitly love the children either. I'm reminded of a moment with my younger son, who, at the age of seven, was in the first grade at a local public school in Santa Cruz. He would come home with homework—inane worksheets like the clown I was directed to color at Riverbend Elementary. As he eased through the work, my son suddenly and emphatically threw his pencil in frustration, looked at me, and said, "Mom, why would anyone think that this matters?" I knew then I'd have to find the resources for him to attend a private school. He wasn't cut out for work that was designed to dampen your spirit and turn your light way down. Is anyone?!

Thankfully, some innovative public schools are demonstrating the efficacy of meditation. At Robert Coleman Elementary in Baltimore, they have a Mindful Moment Room where instead of punishing children who are disruptive or breaking rules, they learn how to self-regulate through meditation. And as a result, detentions are almost non-existent, and attendance and student performance have also increased. Seems like a no-brainer to me. Yet it is the exception, not the rule.

While I'm not conspiratorial, public schooling creates obedient, color-in-the-lines kind of people. People who are connected to themselves and their Divine nature are not easily controlled. For me, Forsyth taught me to see beyond the visual spectrum and tune into the multiple dimensions that are always present.

So, while my memory is fading, given I attended Forsyth over fifty years ago, what I remember is how I felt: safe, loved, and seen. I felt that I mattered, and my psychic self, with all the awareness and connection I had, felt safe there. I looked forward to going. And to this day, I remain friends with almost all my classmates from Forsyth.

Forsyth did so much, but what it couldn't do was help me understand the polarity at home. I have come to understand that contrast is the best teacher. And, for me, contrast abounded in my childhood. At school, I was being filled with love; at home, I experienced violence. The contrast between the respected standing of my father in our community alongside his neglect of me. My mother's remarkable capacity to exude love alongside devastating lows that would keep her in bed for days.

This polarity I didn't know what to do with, how to alchemize it in myself, for years to come.

Chapter 5. Polarity

"Either you just had an orgasm, you are on some kind of drug, or this heart stuff you have been talking about is really working!"

My mother suddenly stopped her manic tirade as we sat in my living room. I was a new mother and my young son, Connor, was finally down for what would always be a brief nap. My mother visited often and on this day was dressed simply in a t-shirt and shorts, which showcased her beautiful legs, more youthful than her movie star face, now weathered with age. A sage suede couch, a large rustic coffee table and an oversized chair that I insisted my husband buy me, given that our son demanded constant nursing, were the only things in the living room of my Tudor-styled home in the diverse town of University City, Missouri, just on the outskirts of downtown St. Louis.

As she ranted, I consciously radiated unconditional love to her—a technique I had cultivated after years of practice. Informed by my early education, personal study, and a dramatic awakening that I'll describe for you a little later, I had mastered how to channel and radiate a laser-focused feeling of unconditional love. This moment with my mother symbolized my most significant life lesson to date: harnessing the power of love to find and sustain my center. I had finally learned how to embody emotional sovereignty in the presence of the extreme energy my mother couldn't regulate within herself. Thankfully on this day, I could inhabit unconditional empathy amidst my mother's unresolved trauma and pain, as she uncontrollably raged at me.

Over the decades, I had witnessed the energetic highs and lows my mother was connected to, which I've come to understand was part of the primordial energy of life itself. Yet without a filter, without conscious discretion in turning it on or off or up or down, she was victimized by it, while also being "charged" by it. It fueled her early success, her clairvoyance, and her capacity to love in magical and uplifting ways. I had dedicated my adult life to figuring out how to channel and regulate the kind of access that my mother and I share, but to do so consciously so that I wouldn't end up ravaged like her.

As a little girl, I sensed, heard and saw things others didn't. I would often feel connected to an invisible, loving presence. During my first year at Forsyth, my teachers called my mother to tell her that I exuded a compassion and empathy for others that they had never witnessed before; they described me as an old soul. I, of course, didn't have that kind of self-awareness so young. All I knew was that I was often frightened by what I saw when I encountered darker energies.

I lived in a world of extremes.

I imprinted my mother's greatness, her magnetic presence, her frequent bouts with deep depression and ravaging darkness, knowing of the remarkable achievements she had created as a young adult, the apparent power she held within her, her capacity for profound wisdom…all while making such tragic choices. I couldn't make sense of it all.

My father's life also stood in great contrast to my life at home. He was rich and famous in our community. I would meet him only for lunch each Sunday, typically at a Michelin-starred, white table-clothed restaurant, which could not have been more different from my life at home with my mother. His house was extravagant and palatial; its regal presence was inspiring. Hand-painted murals reached two stories high and marble floors were perfectly geometric in patterns of black and white. My father's closet was larger than my living room at home. The carriage house, designed to house servants from another time, sat behind his primary residence and was larger and more appointed than the dilapidated home I lived in with my mother and stepfather. My father had confided in me that when he was a little boy living in a boarding house a few streets away from his mansion in Westmorland Place, he proclaimed to himself that when he was a man, that was where he would live. And through his immense will, almost singular focus, intellect, and capacity to stuff his trauma deep in some inner fortress, he had accomplished a powerful, well-resourced, and meaningful life—at least on the surface. Anytime we were out in public, people would enthusiastically and warmly greet him. We couldn't go anywhere without interruption. It was as if he was a celebrity, adorned by fans and getting special treatment wherever we went. He was renowned agent for justice in our community. While he left me alone to navigate the complex trauma of living with my bipolar mother and her violent husband, I didn't feel abandoned by him. He generously supported me financially and was always present when we were together. He had a kind and gentle way about him, and he treated me in our weekly interactions with great love and tenderness. I didn't consciously blame him for what I was enduring at home; instead, I was grateful that his presence, even if it was just weekly, for he provided me ease, resources, and kindness. It wouldn't be until much later that I began to understand the wounding that my relationship with him represented, and once conscious of that, at last I could do the work to heal it.

When you grow up with such extremes, the middle is what you strive for. I wanted a different life, a stable cadence that was trustworthy. Safe.

I found that first through friendship. My childhood best friend, Sharon, lived with her single mother and two sisters. Their home had rhythm, safety, and a kind spirit about it. Sharon's mother taught Tai Chi at our grade school. She was soft in demeanor, supportive, and, most importantly, stable. I spent as much time as possible there, playing on their swing set and eating nectar from the honeysuckle bushes in the backyard—welcome rituals. Our time flew by as we played without worrying about manic disruption or violent outbursts. In the presence of peers or in their homes, I loved experiencing what life without chaos felt like. What safety felt like.

What I then proceeded to do, unconsciously, until the age of twenty-seven was try as hard as I could to find the middle. To find "normal."

I thought that dialing down my power and spiritual access and striving for normality, as proved by social acceptance, would be the answer. I thought that if I were popular with peers, I would have many safe options to spend my time outside my home. As I got older, I sought an exit, leaving home as often as possible and avoiding the trauma that was accumulating inside me by partying with friends and experimenting with drugs and alcohol to numb the pain.

Ultimately, I would learn that to appreciate love, to fully understand its power, you must respect its opposite. You must find a way not to fear the darkness and your shadow, but rather treat it like a welcomed part of you—for it needs your love and acceptance.

But before coming to this understanding, I needed first to experiment, to travel down unconscious life paths and learning through experience that these directions wouldn't lead to healing or wholeness. Since I was yearning for a *conventional* life, in contrast to my home, most choices I made until twenty-seven reflected a traditional path that most people find themselves being encouraged to walk—valuing professional success, material reward, and other such external validation.

Yet, deep in me somewhere, I was still informed by something fundamental to me, my innate intuition—which, ironically, I inherited from my mother. I learned, finally, that the only way to thrive was to heal and do only what was true to me. I became committed to prayer and meditation. I finally came to understand that, given that everything is energy and energy is always seeking homeostasis, my mother's bipolar nature was her system trying to find balance. So instead of leaving it up to my system to mistakenly pursue polarity to come into balance, I learned how to balance myself consciously.

I also learned along the way that there is extreme pressure from conventional forces and those in positions of power who prosper while the rest of us struggle to make ends meet. They need us controlled. They need us not to understand the power we have to create. They need us to believe that God, that Divine power, is outside of us. So they teach that God is not within but is an old, angry, judgmental man who tracks who is naughty and punishes us for our sins.

But to *sin*, in Aramaic, the language that the word derives from simply means to "miss the mark." To make a mistake. I invite you to reassess how you have been programmed by institutional forces designed to keep you obedient and afraid. What if in your beating heart resides your infinite, eternal soul? An energy so powerful it never dies, just changes form, as the laws of physics teach us. What if you spent time there daily, focusing your breath and consciously trying to connect to the power within you? What if, as you consciously connected to feelings of love and gratitude every day, that access grew, widened, and deepened? What if, with practice, you knew how to manifest your heart's desire? What if you knew how to use the energy of love to heal all the dark, wounded places within? What then?

You would then have mastery of yourself. You would know how to regulate the energy within you. You wouldn't be a victim of everyday stresses. You wouldn't need your system to adapt to try and find balance, swinging you down or up in its attempts to keep you whole. You would be in charge of you.

By watching the miss-the-mark moments of my parents, extended family, peers, and, most importantly, myself, I learned that in my core was a center I needed to cultivate if I was going to thrive. This center was named at Forsyth, where I was first taught that love is the most powerful energy available to us. The preparation is taxing, like baking a layer cake, but the reward is rich, flavorful, and yummy, just like the life you can create from a coherent, grateful heart. The dark forces at work do not want you to know how powerful you actually are. They do not want you to be integrated, but rather, polarized and divided.

And so, a lifetime of trauma, turbulence, and extremes preceded my capacity to self-regulate and embody sovereignty in this way. Each phase of my life taught me something essential for my healing. As I reflect on it all—each phase, each moment of trauma, each mistake I made—I see how my resolution wove all these moments into the bigger purpose for my life.

As I sat in my living room, radiating love towards my mother that day, I saw it all so clearly. In those moments of ravaging darkness, my mother needed love. And in receiving the energy I was radiating to her system, she could come into balance.

She abruptly stopped talking. She could feel what I was sending her, and she quieted upon receipt. Feeling loved and feeling the love, she, too, found her center. Even if only for a moment or two.

Chapter 6. Achieve

When it's 100 degrees and 99% humidity, you find refuge. It was the summer before my senior year in high school and I wanted to escape the sweltering St. Louis heat. I carefully placed a bed sheet on the air conditioning vent of my bedroom, placing as many books as I could gather off my bookshelves to secure the perimeter to create a cold, safe fort. As I lay on my back, daydreaming of winter days with my best friend and neighbor Heidi sledding, making snow ice cream, staying out until our fingers began to lose feeling, the cold air began to make the bed sheet rise. I finally grew comfortable. Then, in the quiet, with only the sound of the air conditioner as my companion, a quiet inner voice that I had learned to trust spoke.

"It's time, Regan. Time to fully apply yourself, do as you're told at school. Study. Do your homework. Work hard."

And so, when I entered my senior year that fall, and for the first time since leaving Forsyth at age eleven, I surrendered almost without exception, to the expectations of my high school. I earned straight A's that year—with the exception of an English class I walked out of in protest of the poor teaching, for which I received an F. Ironically, I didn't even need the English credit to graduate. I guess my rebellious spirit couldn't be completely tamed, despite my best efforts. For reasons I am still not certain of, the administrators at my high school treated me differently from my peers. One memory stands out that reflected this. On a sunny spring day, prior to committing to excellence as my inner guidance demanded, I confidently walked out the front door of my high school. I was skipping another mediocre, mind numbing class. I knew as I walked that the administrators were lined up outside attempting to catch truants red handed. But instead they smiled broadly at me as they saw me and asked me where I was going. I quickly answered, "I am heading to Jack in the Box for a snack." They then asked me if I would bring them back Danishes and coffee and gave me $20. My friends had always commented that rules just didn't seem to apply to me. I had had over 300 absences in high school and there was never a letter or phone call received. My teachers would remark often about "my potential" and I would quickly respond that they frankly knew nothing about it or me. I was somewhat aware that I radiated fearlessness and supreme confidence. Years later in my mid-twenties, I attended a wedding of a dear friend whose father was a local superintendent for a large suburban school district. As I sat in the cocktail lounge at the reception sipping on a martini, I saw in the distance my former high school principal. I cupped my hands to try and yell over the conversations that were increasing in volume, the mood festive. "Dr. Katsaras, is that you?" He looked blankly at me, clearly not recognizing me. My pixie haircut was quite the contrast to the long, loosely curled hair I had in high school. "It's me. Regan Caruthers!" I then saw him take an exaggerated deep breath as he approached me. As he looked at me with a mix of love and apprehension he shared, "We simply didn't know what to do with you." I replied, "Well, that would have been a valuable conversation to have." We spoke for a few minutes and I walked away still not understanding what he had meant. And while I have no way of knowing precisely why, my sense of personal power and lack of unearned respect for conventional authority came from my unconscious relationship with Divine forces that had been fostered at Forsyth. When you can sense the truth of who you are the only authority that seems worthy of your devotion is God.

Throughout my adolescence, I hadn't reflected much on how my intuition was guiding me, how it had been fostered at Forsyth School, how that spiritual connection was affecting me, or how it had impacted my friends in high school. I must have dialed it down so far to fit in that I assumed it was gone entirely.

* * *

"Regan, if you wouldn't mind, I'd like to speak to you privately? Can we find a quiet place to talk?"

My high school friend, Howie, struggled to raise his voice loud enough so I could hear him over the celebratory background of our 25th high school reunion. He then added, "I did mention to my wife that we were going to spend some private time together." Intrigued by his request, I followed him out of the banquet hall. We found a quiet spot to sit. His face was serious. I was a bit baffled, not knowing what was driving his desire to talk. Then, with emotion all over his face, he began. "I know I am the man that I am, the kind of committed husband and father, because of you and what you taught me about emotional intimacy back in high school. You showed us all how to connect with honesty and authenticity. I felt safe to be myself with you, to be vulnerable and tender. You saw me and what you embodied was different from our peers. Your presence was wise, you seemed connected to something and that something enabled me to be *me* when I was with you. Your directness was never mean, always loving. Now as a man, I am able to communicate with honesty and directness and my heart is open and vulnerable. I learned how to do that from you." He went on, describing moments in junior high and high school with great detail that he had been carrying with him all these years.

And I had no memory of any of it. I thought of one of my favorite sayings of my mother, "I don't know what I just said, but I really meant it!" I realized that, even as a distracted and traumatized adolescent, I must have still been unconsciously connected to a higher intelligence within me, a wisdom guiding me in my interactions with my peers. I was deeply grateful that Howie shared what he did with me. I told him I was happy knowing I had been of service to him, even if I didn't remember a single thing he had brought up from our pasts.

But when I do look at my adolescent past, one key moment of intuitive insight glimmers back at me.

I was in middle school and my mother was driving me to an orthodontist appointment. I was staring out the car window, daydreaming in the rare quiet, when suddenly I heard the counsel of a clear, caring voice telling me to repeat the ninth grade. I was a year ahead of my peers academically, given the self-paced nature of Forsyth, and I was struggling to fit in socially. I was small, physically developing much later than my peers, and was frequently bullied, mostly by boys. So the guidance to stay back a year and catch up with myself immediately resonated with me. There was no inner deliberation; I knew in my heart it was right and I quickly shared it with my mom, my loving confidant, as she drove.

Without hesitation, as if she too knew the rightness of it, she said, "Well, dear I don't know a thing about how to do that, but you have my full support."

A month later, at the age of 13, I found myself presenting to the Parkway School District's Board of Education. Since there was no policy mechanism to allow a student in good academic standing to stay back, I needed to persuade them that it was in my best interest. I was successful in my pitch to them and this created a turning point in my adolescent life. In my second ninth grade year, I worked for the administration, took all electives, and was given the freedom of all lunch hours to fill the day, which provided me lots of time to socialize and build new relationships. I wanted nothing else than to thrive socially. Although my mother continued to be supportive in many ways, she was also regularly hospitalized for either mania or depression. Her husband Joe's drunken tirades intensified, creating such a hostile and unpredictably frightening home that I longed for and needed the safety and serenity found in the homes of others when in the care of my friends' parents. That year I was invited to parties, became popular with peers, and enjoyed competitive track and cheerleading. For the first time since leaving Forsyth, I felt happy and safe in school.

After leaving Forsyth before enrolling in public school, I had been accepted to begin seventh grade at the elite John Burroughs School, a school for St. Louis' brightest. Graduates of Burroughs most often attended the Ivy Leagues. After successfully passing their IQ test, meeting their expectations in the admissions interview, and passing their rigorous entrance exam, my father's standing in the community propelled this unquestioned next step and my life was now being directed by his expectations.

And I hated every minute of it. The days at John Burroughs, which were ten class-periods long, stood in stark contrast to Forsyth. Come winter, I would leave school in the dark, for the class day ended at 4:17. My peers were cliquey and mean. The values were all about achievement and how much money your father made. When I demanded, after one year, to go to public school, thankfully my father conceded. It helped that the $4,000 yearly tuition in 1978 didn't land well with his third wife. I started public school the following year.

Public school was better than it would have been at John Burroughs, and despite the wisdom of repeating the ninth grade, my home life had me on the run. Throughout, I was focused on exiting. Exiting my inner pain, exiting through consistent absences the mediocrity of some of my teachers as I struggled to complete inane homework assignments and rarely if ever studied for exams.

I often felt alone, sad, and overwhelmed inside, though on the outside I appeared to be thriving. Popular with peers yet feeling very much alone.

At least I had Heidi, my next-door neighbor. As we grew into teens, we partied a lot. We would skim liquor off the many bottles that stood almost ceremonially in her basement bar, combining all the skimmed liquors into a secret Tupperware container. My job was to bring the exotic fruit juices that were always available at my house as mixers. Her father was in poor health, his heart clogged from a bad diet and too much alcohol. Her mother had left him and Heidi was put into the position of taking care of him, the house, and her younger sister. Our weekends were spent in *exit*. Alcohol and marijuana provided release from the trauma of both of our homes. We would find the shade and shelter of a grove of pines and sit together talking, laughing, and numbing ourselves. Heidi and I needed each other.

Riding the momentum of academic excellence in senior year after heeding my inner guidance, I applied to the University of Missouri with the intention of studying pre-law. I didn't consider anywhere else. Many of my high school friends were attending college there, but the real, unconscious reason I wanted to stay close to home was to be close to my mother, to support her ups, but mostly her downs.

College came easy to me. I earned a 3.94 GPA my first year. Ironically, I earned a B in a physical education class called, *Figure Improvement*. Hard to believe that in 1985 there would be such a class. Perfectionism had taken over my system. I was significantly underweight due to anorexia, which is all about gaining control, and had been hospitalized. Having missed too many Figure Improvement classes, even though the instructor knew it was due to being hospitalized for anorexia, I was given a B. Being in the hospital was so alarming that once discharged I began to eat again, though I was still compulsively driven. I intended to make up for lost time and get my academic life on track. Striving as I did was deeply comforting; I felt in control. Because my home life had felt so out of control for so long, perfection felt soothing to me. I was quickly developing an ethos that control and achievement would create safety.

This ethos would only become stronger and stronger in the years that followed, catapulting me into corporate achievements that would capitalize on this drive in me. I would also learn, in time, that only way to feel safe was to heal my deeply traumatized inner child. Yet in my early twenties my solution was achievement and a commitment to excellence.

Chapter 7. Freedom Through Work

I pulled into the driveway of my father's country estate, my handsome fiancé, Michael, by my side, with an ebullient sense of pride. The driveway stretched a quarter mile or so and majestic pines perfectly framed the asphalt. I peered through the trees to see the first house, sitting back from the road that housed the caretaker who cared for the 135 acres in exchange for this quaint, quiet place to live. We were surrounded by rolling pasture, horses grazing, two spring-fed lakes, and five other homes built with knotted pine. "The farm," as we called the estate, was another symbol of my father's success and his desire for opulence.

I sped up. I couldn't wait to show my Dad the company car I had been given. It was a stately steel grey and looked a bit like a top hat—likely better suited for a grandparent than a twenty-three-year-old woman. I didn't care that the car didn't suit my youth, it was mine; a vehicle I would use to travel my territory as a sales representative for Prentice Hall, an academic publisher.

Shortly after graduating college with honors, I had endured nine interviews with a new, young manager who had finally made the decision to hire me. I was ecstatic about my new career; it fit my intellect and social intelligence like a glove.

As I approached the main house, I exited the car and ran to the back where my father, his son, my half-brother Rex, with his wife

Anna and their young children, were gathered around the pool. A tension always ran through these gatherings. My half-brother didn't like spending time there; he held deep resentment toward our father and couldn't stand to be around our father's fourth wife, Rachel. Rex is twenty-two years older than me. We weren't close, in fact back then his presence was rather difficult to tolerate. Our perceptions of our father were as if we truly had different dads. Rex saw my father as corrupt at work and negligent of us, his children. I experienced a kind, present father who always insured I had financial resources and his emotional support, even if it was only weekly. I always chose to ignore the underlying tension and was just happy to see my sweet dad. While my dad had only seen me once a week my entire life, with the exception of a few vacations we had taken together, a deep bond had formed through the unconditional love we felt for each other. He was always kind to me. His stature in our community gave me a sense of confidence and prominence.

And I couldn't wait to tell him all about my new job. "Dad, I got it! I'm going to work as a sales representative for Prentice Hall! This is the new car they gave me. I also get a 401K and health insurance!" His eyes beamed with pride as I explained my responsibilities and how I would be traveling across my Midwest territory selling textbooks to college instructors who taught the trades. His enthusiasm for my new career was sincere; I could sense he was proud of me. My mother once told me that when I was little, he looked at her wistfully one day and said, "If only Regan's brain was in her brother's body." He wasn't a chauvinist, his perception wasn't mean spirited. He simply had been born in 1923 and grew up in a time when women had few opportunities outside the home. He truly believed that my options would be inherently limited because I was female. Frankly, he wasn't wrong.

I wanted nothing more than to be the grown up I suddenly seemed to be. I was driven to create a stable life, free of turbulence, abundant in financial ease. While I have no way of truly knowing, I believe my self-confidence and sense of personal power at this stage of life came from three sources: my mother's magnetic love, my early spiritual education long forgotten, and my father's prominence.

I thrived at work. Driving my Dodge Dynasty along rural highways, windows all down, music blaring from the modest speakers, the wind in my hair, I felt free. Free to create a life on my own terms, defined by my productivity and my corporate ascension. My first year at Prentice Hall I had a sixty-four percent increase in sales—frankly unheard of in terms of sales growth. I was quickly building a professional reputation of high performance.

My mentor, who had recently been promoted to be my district manager and was the one who hired me, trained me so well. She and I developed a deep friendship. In fact, she remains one of my closest friends, more than thirty years later. When she worked with me in the field, she marveled at the ease of my selling, telling me once after a day of work together that I was the first person she had ever worked with where she had nothing to add. I loved the freedom I found in working, the annual bonuses, and the professional praise I received by anyone who joined me for a day's work in the field. I thought I had command of myself. I thought I was thriving. The false ethos that professional advancement would lead to emotional safety drove my efforts.

I ended my time at Prentice Hall two years after starting there to take a promotion with a competitor. My last year there, unbeknownst to me, I was the number one sales representative for my division.

I had been wooed away by the former vice president of sales for Prentice Hall, who had left to join a competitor, also bringing a top-performing regional manager with him. As they built their new management team, they decided that recruiting me was in their strategic interest. When they called asking if I was interested in joining them, I felt immediately excited and eager for advancement. I had great respect for them both and we had a deep connection; they were people I trusted. I knew I could learn a great deal by working for them directly.

The position they offered me had many dimensions. Primarily I was the closer, the one to join the sales representative in the field and make final presentations to faculty to close priority business for the company. The role was also recruiter and teacher—specifically teaching sales representatives how to be strong performers. And finally, my new role included business development. Publishing was beginning to change at this time. There was pressure to figure out how the Internet and technology in general was going to impact the business, so I was also asked to scout for partnerships and new technology that could help the company leap. The intense enthusiasm I felt for this new role was all consuming.

This time I was given a sportier car, a Mazda 626. As I drove around, marveling at the oscillating air-conditioning vents, the sunroof, the leather seats and the automatic everything. I felt like I had arrived. I was twenty-five years old and responsible for over $12 million in revenue for the company. The trauma of my past and my early spiritual education were faint in my awareness; in fact I didn't reflect on any of that. I was just charging ahead as fast as I could move.

***

I rushed into the neighborhood copy shop, frantic, as I impatiently waited for the clerk. My body was buzzing with stress. All suited up, elegantly dressed, and running late, I had a plane to catch and needed the clerk to collect the presentation binder I had ordered with rapid speed. I forced myself to be kind; if I had been authentic, I would have screamed at her to hurry up. Instead I stood there, my body humming with an intensity that the clerk could sense. We had had many encounters before and she was always helpful and informed about my varying copy needs, putting presentations together for me that would guide my interactions in some distant Midwestern college town.

"Look at you, Ms. Regan, working yourself to death to make someone else a lot of money." She looked at me with empathetic concern and simple wisdom. I paused, smiled at her, and took a deep breath. I recognized the truth of what she had said; yet I impatiently charged on.

As I sat on the plane heading to close the calculus business at the University of Iowa, I reflected on her comment. She was right. I was spiraling, consumed with a stress that felt out of control. Often I would wake up to an alarm in my hotel room and needed to think for a minute before remembering which city I was in.

I began to consider that my professional life was not sustainable.

A few weeks later, my fiancé returned to our modest apartment after a day's work. He had just attended a luncheon hosted by the Missouri Round Table, a venue where entrepreneurs would pitch business ideas to local financiers for investment. He had heard a presentation from a local college professor whose family was the largest shareholder in Anheuser-Busch. This professor-turned-entrepreneur had access to abundant family resources, which had funded his business to date. He demonstrated a prototype of his invention—what we now would recognize as a Kindle or an early-model iPad. It was 1992 and the Internet was still in development, not yet something the average person was using. He explained his plan to partner with Hughes Aircraft to support satellite delivery of content that this prototyped device would consume.

As Michael shared this with me, I had an immediate sense that this invention mattered and could transform the distribution of content. I quickly made arrangements to meet with the inventor and began to develop a trusted relationship with him. He relied on me to better understand the publishing industry and I sensed that what he had invented was exactly the kind of innovation my company asked me to scout. After I felt I had learned enough about this transformative technology, I drafted a proposal for the CFO, recommending that my employer, a publisher with offices across the globe, make a strategic investment in this young entrepreneur who had the first patent on the eBook. I expended tremendous energy to put together my proposal. Inexperienced at anything like this, I was now presenting to company executives many layers above my management team.

Their response to me was laughable. They declined, remarking that they didn't think the market would adopt anything besides the desktop or laptop computer, and if for some unlikely reason the market did adopt such technology, they weren't at risk by not investing. The executives treated me with a kind of sexist and patronizing awe. *This beautiful young woman has some balls!* They were condescending in their tone to me, as if I didn't have the chops or the business maturity to make any kind of investment recommendation. In April of 2010, *eighteen* years after my company rejected my proposal, Steve Jobs released the first version of the iPad that would revolutionize the publishing industry and change reading habits across the globe. Imagine if the executives had taken my proposal seriously, the company would have been on the leading edge of digital content distribution. I often wonder if I had looked like them—a middle-aged white man with a belly made from neglect, alcohol and cigarettes, the staples of the publishing industry, with no other experience than publishing books—would they have listened to me? I'll never know.

The mix of the rejection of my proposal, the feedback from the copy shop clerk, and the inhumane actions of many colleagues at work who not only patronized me, but were also sexually harassing me, began to build a different kind of fire inside me. And while I had no conscious idea or sense at the time, what was soon to transpire would radically change my life, my priorities, and my sense of self. Most importantly, it would catalyze my healing and commitment to helping others heal.

Chapter 8. **Awakening**

I had learned from Marion, my distant Dutch cousin, some thirty years after beginning my publishing career, that the Viewegs, my Dutch paternal line, had founded Vieweg Publishing in the late 1700s. So, just like the trauma of my ancestors lived in my cells, so apparently did my seeking a publishing career in 1990. In just a few intense years of work, in the industry that apparently lived somewhere in my DNA, I found myself worn down and worn out. In quiet moments often fueled by nicotine, the voice of the copy clerk still echoed in my mind.

In early January of 1994, I traveled to San Francisco for a national sales meeting with my global publisher. My hotel suite was spacious and comfortable and I appreciated the presence of alcohol in the mini bar to numb my pain. I had a lot to process.

Shortly after I arrived at the meeting that morning, I learned that the VP of Sales—my original recruiter, mentor, and friend—had been fired without cause. I had been hired to be part of a new management initiative. Its purpose was to evolve the company from an almost solely editorial focus to one that shifted resources and operational focus to sales and marketing. Executives and managers who had been there for decades greeted my new team with open hostility. At meetings, as soon as they learned that I was part of the new team, they would abruptly walk away. I remember once extending my hand to shake one of the editorial leaders and mid-handshake, as soon as he heard my name, he abruptly dropped my hand, turned and walked the other direction. Quickly, as if I had some kind of disease he could catch. These regressive forces were creating a hostile environment and it was clear they weren't interested in making any substantive changes to their business practices. My team was the minority, outnumbered, and I was losing hope that any real change would occur.

Midweek my manager called to see if I wanted to come to her suite. We sat, late into the night, talking about the drama of the meeting. She seemed raw with grief and anger as we talked like old girlfriends as opposed to work colleagues. And then she broke, tears rolling down her cheeks, as she told me she had been raped. My heart bled with grief for her. The brutality of what she went through and the fact that anyone could be capable of such brutality filled me with rage, deep fear, and an intense desire to act. She never told me who it was, but what I felt was that some kind of values-based red line had been crossed.

Countless times, I had witnessed men at work demeaning me and other female colleagues; this company and its regressive forces were right out of *Mad Men*. My desire to "succeed," to climb the corporate mountaintop, seemed unimportant now. The rape, the unjust firing, the rejection of my proposal, the cruelty I witnessed, how people were acculturated to behave when unconsciously afraid of change, created a response within me that felt like mania.

I thought of my mother. *Was this how she felt? Is this what happens when you witness one too many unjust acts?*

For the rest of the trip, leading meeting sessions and interacting with colleagues during social events became almost unbearable. Incessant smoking and drinking were not enough to numb my pain. I remember bringing holiday photos of my husband, parents, and dear friends with me to an evening cocktail party. I looked at myself in those photos—radiant and surrounded by love—as I drank to numb myself. I needed the reminder of seeing me joyful and radiant with possibility in the photos, qualities that seemed so distant at work. One of the calculus editors that I worked with glanced at one of the photos and remarked, "Do you ever feel like you chose the wrong career? Shouldn't you have been a model?" He said it snarkily, with an intellectual affectation. Here I had helped make his book a bestseller and this is how he speaks to me? I wanted to punch him, but instead smiled and walked away.

As the toxic pressures continued to accumulate in my system, I was grateful knowing that my childhood best friend Heidi was coming to stay with me in my suite. Heidi had just graduated from the Culinary Institute of America in New York and was heading my way to interview for a job at the famed Boulevard restaurant, a renowned San Francisco eatery. I was comforted knowing Heidi was on her way; I longed for the comfort of someone I could trust.

When she arrived, she greeted me with a gift: *A Return to Love* by Marianne Williamson. I was touched by her sentiment and as I opened the book, I quickly glanced at the introduction: "When we were born, we were programmed perfectly. We had a natural tendency to focus on love. Our imaginations were creative and flourishing, and we knew how to use them. We were connected to a world much richer than the one we connect to now, a world full of enchantment and a sense of the miraculous."

I looked up at Heidi and said, "Thank you. I love you, but I don't have time for this." And off I went to lead my next session.

That night, overtaken by manic exhaustion, I was glad to know that Heidi was going to go out to experience the city, have some cocktails, and socialize. I went to bed fatigued. I wasn't prayerful. I wasn't grateful. I had no spiritual practice. I was tired, angry, exhausted, and felt surrounded by enemies who sought to do me harm. All I wanted was a decent night's sleep. A few hours later in the dark of night, I woke up with a familiar sense of terror, which felt reminiscent of times alone in bed as a child. Of what I had seen in the basement of my mother's house. The terror awakened me from a deep sleep and I knew as I opened my eyes that someone—or something—was in my room. I could feel him before I could see him.

There, standing at the end of my bed, was the same entity I saw often as a young girl, the one I had said a dramatic goodbye to at the age of nine as I fled up my basement steps. I recognized him immediately. He stood with arms crossed, as if studying me. His hair grazing his shoulders, a red headband across his forehead looking like someone better suited for Woodstock than my hotel suite. Out of some fundamental extinct I said to him, "Oh, it's only you. I am not afraid of you." I then closed my eyes and fell back asleep.

As I opened my eyes the next morning, I was met by feelings that are hard to put into words. I felt a deep, complete peace, a profound feeling of oneness, and love for all. I harbored no ill will for my colleagues; instead I loved them, forgave them, and understood them. I knew in the cells of my being that the choices they had made were just expressions of fear and internal suffering. I understood everything as if I was clearly connected to an intelligence beyond my physical self. And I knew this feeling. It predominated my young life. Everything made sense. I understood my mother, my stepfather who was abusive to his son, and me. I knew, again, that the only reason we exist is to learn to love and to understand how we are all connected to each other and to the larger force that created us. I understood fully that fear is an illusion and, as long as we fear, we can't love. I knew that morning, and know it still, that our collective task is to transmute suffering by accessing the healing energy of love.

I had returned to love. I was no longer asleep.

Not knowing how long this unexplainable understanding would last, I longed to reach my mother back in St. Louis and tell her everything I was sensing. Unlike any other time before, I couldn't reach her by phone, nor could I reach my husband or father. The only person who picked up my call was Joe, my stepfather, who had been the primary source of fear, violence, and chaos for most of my life. And now I felt nothing but love for him. I understood him and the pain that drove his actions. As he answered the phone, a presence within me began to speak and tell him the larger picture. I wanted to let him know how much I loved him and that I had nothing but complete forgiveness for him. I wasn't speaking, not Regan; it was as if God himself was talking through me. "The purpose of living is to learn how to Love, to return to Love, for it's what we are, there is no other purpose."

Joe listened, and then dropped the phone. I heard it scuffle to the ground. A few seconds later, phone back in hand, he said, "Well, Blonde Beauty, I have no explanation for this, but a golden eagle just landed on the top of the crabapple tree in the backyard." Then another pause, a phone drop, then he returned seconds later again. "I don't understand what I'm seeing, but a red fox is now at the base of this tree, looking up at the eagle." Joe has Comanche ancestry and in the Native American tradition, the eagle and red fox are powerful symbols. The eagle is the most revered animal, a symbol of what is highest, bravest, strongest and holiest, thus the closest animal to the Divine itself. The fox represents a wise and noble messenger. So somehow these symbols, resonant with his ancestral traditions, appeared seemingly out of nowhere and I think helped Joe understand the power he was experiencing.

From that moment to now, thirty years later, Joe is a different man: kind, gentle, caring, loving, and generous in his actions. The energy of Divine love, which I had voiced and embodied during that phone call, changed him. The abuse he had suffered as a child, which drove his adult behaviors, no longer ruled him. Having been fully loved, he could heal. The energy of Divine love had traveled thousands of miles over the phone lines to him and he was forever different. I was changed too.

Upon returning to St. Louis, I greeted my husband with a feeling of endless love. The love I felt for him was beyond words, beyond what I had ever known. I shared with him what had happened to me in San Francisco; he met the change in me with loving acceptance. He didn't deny in any way what I had experienced; he seemed to understand the truth of what I now embodied for it mirrored his personal study. Years earlier when we first fell in love it was he who introduced me to Carlos Castaneda. It was he who was striving to understand the mystical. Michael held great capacity within him. Though like my mother he struggled to regulate it within himself. That night, we conceived our first son, Connor, in the most ecstatic lovemaking we had yet experienced. The moment our son's spirit entered my body, I knew it and I greeted him. I felt I knew him already and was ready to bring him into this world. I sensed he would be a healer and a teacher and help raise the consciousness of the planet at what felt like a critical time. My elevated consciousness and feelings of oneness and unconditional love for all lasted for about three years and brought immense healing and new opportunities for my life and work.

Now back home in St. Louis, and newly pregnant, my awakened state brought a driven fearlessness for creating change at work by speaking authentically about how toxic the work environment was—though not from a place a judgment, for I knew the behaviors I witnessed were born from fear and trauma. I began a quest to expose the ethical breaches of my workplace leadership and became an outspoken critic of what I was seeing. I penned a letter to the CEO of the entire global enterprise, not breaking any confidences from colleagues, but referencing the misdeeds at the top. There were plenty to reference.

Upon receipt, the CEO flew me out to headquarters, where I led a frank discussion about how fear of change can have people do unspeakable things. I challenged him to do something about it. But nothing was done; instead I saw a restructuring of the company, which eliminated the region that my raped mentor had led, thus forcing her out. I then brought my father into the mix to represent three women in Equal Employment Opportunity Commission lawsuits, supported by a federal agency created to enforce civil rights laws protecting employees from workplace discrimination. These lawsuits centered on the sexual harassment of women who had been treated with such disregard and inhumanity.

My reputation at work was now not about my high performance. I was perceived as a threat. Since I was pregnant, their choices were constrained and they knew it. What I then experienced was surreal. I simply stopped getting any corporate mail and sales reports were no longer accessible to me. They made no announcement, they simply wanted me mute. I spent the next nine months doing nothing at work other than counseling colleagues on the phone and spending my time nurturing my developing baby and basking in the awakened state that was still deeply present.

After my son arrived and my maternity leave ended, I resigned. Then, come the end of the calendar year, months after my resignation, I received a bonus check. I hadn't done any work that year. I had no idea how they could have calculated bonus to my efforts given that I hadn't traveled, closed any business, or contributed to revenue in any way. When I opened the envelope to see the substantial bonus I received, I sensed a payoff.

I proclaimed to myself in that moment that I would now live a life of service, teaching people what I knew to be true. I had seen up close how stress compromises people's capacity to think strategically and clearly. I had witnessed how untended wounds show up at work, and God knows I knew how that showed up at home. Fear and trauma can have people do unspeakable things. I wanted to help people understand how connecting to love and healing their trauma can not only change one's life, it can also create excellence at work and enable you to have greater resilience to navigate life's complexities.

For three years after my dramatic awakening, my days were filled with miracles but my nights quickly became filled with terror. I was tasked with learning how to reconcile what felt like intense inner duality. A polarity really, just like I had known as a child. What I now understand is all the trauma of my past and the choice I made to greet my fear with a sense of sovereignty rather than emotional panic when I woke up to see my "visitor" at the end of the bed had created the conditions within myself for a dramatic shift. Now my task was how to integrate my changed state of being into a world that hadn't changed.

But before I could integrate my awakened consciousness and understanding, I needed first to truly learn how to confront the darkness that was visiting me night after night, just as it had when I was little.

The best way I can describe what I was experiencing is to relate it to *Star Wars* when Luke Skywalker was training to be a Jedi. As Luke trains, he confronts Darth Vader in a dark tunnel. There, his fear creates a simulation of what he needs to confront. I sensed that the darkness I was experiencing was there to teach me something, yet I didn't yet know what I needed to learn or how to Jedi my way through it. What I now understand is that this part of my healing journey was the most critical. Being able to be sovereign, to be able to love the darkness not just the light, to be liberated from fear would require that I find a way to love and accept darkness. Darkness within myself, some of which I inherited through ancestral trauma, some through direct experience as a reflection of my past actions, and darkness that operated in the world.

"If you want to be an instrument of the light, you must understand and accept your own darkness," a trusted voice within said clearly as I drove my toddler to the park one beautiful spring day. I had asked my guides about the purpose of my recent experiences that were the polar opposite of how I felt during the daylight;

unconditional immense love by day, ravaging fear at night as I lay sleeplessly in bed. The darkness I was experiencing now was even more terrifying than what I had seen as a kid, which is saying a lot. Once I fell asleep, I would abruptly awaken to find myself surrounded by dark forces. These forces I could feel and see. They were fiery red and smoky black and they terrified me. Sometimes I would hear a strong whooshing sound, like a powerful wind between my ears. As these entities surrounded me, I would be pulled from my body against my will and my spirit would travel to unrecognizable places, like I was touring the dark, terrifying corners of the universe—akin to finding yourself lost driving through violent ghettos in a city. Some nights I would have to muster all my will to return to myself. I would see myself lying in bed and have to exert all personal force to return.

I felt completely alone in this, for who could possibly understand it? Who could provide me counsel to assist in learning how to navigate what felt like an initiation? I was acutely aware that if I confided in a mental health professional I would have been diagnosed with some kind of psychosis. I knew in my heart that nothing was wrong, that nothing needed to be fixed; I just needed to trust in what was emerging within me and find social support to guide my process. Somehow.

Thankfully I found someone: the minister at the local Unity Church where Forsyth School began. Returning there felt like I was returning to something fundamental within me, namely the profound spiritual teachings that had predominated my school days as an elementary school student. Like me, the minister, Lawrence, was having spontaneous experiences that he described as shamanic journeying. We supported each other. We upheld our sanity and learned together how to interact with forces that were trying to teach us something essential. We would meet on Wednesday evenings, confiding in each other. Through this expansive connection I felt like at least I had one person who understood and could meet me where I was. He and I would practice together as we learned how to navigate with more mastery other dimensions of time and space. We would agree to meet at a certain time in the morning. I would fall deep in a meditative state and with abiding faith, exit my body to meet him. Soul to soul, spirit to spirit. The process felt familiar. Just as yogis experienced the great and final Samadhi, I was learning how to fully let go and trust that the Divine had my back. Exiting my body at will was one of the most profound experiences of my young life for once experienced you have no fear of death. I knew without any doubt after experiencing this that I was energy temporarily housed in something we call the body.

As time passed and with more practice, I also learned how to not fear the darkness that was visiting me night after night. Similar to how I responded to the entity that greeted me in my San Francisco hotel suite, I learned how to first feel neutral in the presence of profound darkness. Then, in time, I learned how to radiate love to these forces, just as I had radiated love to my mother that afternoon in my living room, when she was overcome by dark, manic energy. And once I mastered being able to love the darkness, the visitations stopped.

I've often thought if I had been able to, as young girl, love my visitors instead of being terrified by them that my awakening could have happened earlier. I found myself grateful for my visitors for they had taught me the most profound lesson: that the energy of love, particularly when confronted with darkness, can transmute anything.

In the years that followed, as my ecstatic, feel-only-love consciousness by day faded, I would eventually learn how to integrate it all, alchemizing my life and the lives of my ancestors into meaning, purpose, and finally inner peace. While I was not aware of this at this time, the pull of the external world, the need to make a living, parent, and live in this modern world, would diminish my connection to this ecstatic state. Each choice I made not to nurture and practice cultivating higher awareness led, of course, to lower awareness and lower states of consciousness. Time spent not meditating, not praying, not connecting to my higher self led me slowly, without conscious awareness, to choices informed by former habits and former ways of being.

Chapter 9. Trauma

In the years following my awakening, my consciousness no longer could sustain feelings of oneness and deeply felt Divine presence, so I found myself having to re-commit to healing. I realized that conscious healing was an ongoing process. That even though I had experienced a profound transformation, finding my way back to that state of awareness required me to experiment, to try new modalities of healing. I knew that attaining a higher state of consciousness required consistent effort, though I often lacked the self-discipline needed to sustain higher awareness. One modality, network chiropractic, held deep resonance for me. I had begun seeing a network chiropractor soon after my awakening in St. Louis and now years later had found remarkable network chiropractors in Santa Cruz.

I lay on my chiropractor's table hearing the moans and exhales of the other patients in the room—the kind of chiropractic work I was drawn to happened in community. The others were dressed in typical Santa Cruz garb, the women wearing flowing skirts and beaded halter-tops, as if they were sitting on the lawn of a Grateful Dead concert. While I assumed we valued the same things—personal growth, healing, organic food, and shared understanding that our issues lived in our tissues—you would have never assumed that by my attire. Usually I was dressed like the businessperson I was at the time, a successful, middle-aged business development executive. Today, my off-work uniform was as usual, yoga pants and a modest workout top.

The gentle touches of my network chiropractor always yielded release, and on this day, the release would yield remembering. I was a committed recipient, knowing that as I unwound my spine and nervous system, I was also releasing cellular memories—moments when I felt scared, abandoned, unsafe, and unsure. But in order to release trauma, I knew I first needed to tap into the felt experience—like threading a needle, but the needle is the emotion and you must enter into its center and be willing to feel its depth. Ian, my chiropractor, would adjust me with faint touch, directing me to breathe where he touched along my spine.

That particular day, I don't remember where his touch was on my body at that moment but as I deeply exhaled, I was transported back in time.

I was two years old, frightened beyond what I can articulate here on the page. Paramedics had arrived, put my mother on a gurney, and were taking her away from our stately condo. I was screaming, sensing that my mother was in grave danger. My mother, desperately sad and without hope, had consumed pills with the intent to end her life. She and I lived alone. She had kicked my father out, having learned of his infidelity with the help of a private detective she had hired, and she wanted it all to end. Even her vast love for me was not enough to keep her wanting to live.

Then the memory flashed of living with family friends who volunteered to take care of me as my mother recovered in the hospital. I felt lost, uncertain, and didn't really understand where my mother was or why she was away; all I knew was that I missed her more than anything and wanted to see her. See her strikingly beautiful red hair in a classic seventies flip, always dressed as if she had somewhere important to go. She would sit on the end of the turquoise chaise lounge and clap her hands, "A hug, a kiss, and a squeeze, hurry, hurry!"

In that moment on the chiropractor's table, I remembered how her love felt. I flashed on being a teen on her king-sized bed made with ivory stained wood, her headboard elaborately carved in circular shapes, a piece of art really, that was a relic from another time when she was married to my father and had financial ease, but little else. Her embrace, the warmth of her breath, and the magnitude of the energy she was connected to in those moments when she held me close were moments where I felt infinitely loved and safe, regardless of the circumstances that surrounded us.

I wept with abandon on the chiropractor's table, a bit self-conscious of the hugeness of what I was releasing since other people were just a table away, but equally committed to feeling it all so I could finally let it go.

Up until that moment, I had no conscious memory of my mother's suicide attempt, nor did I ever consciously think about it, though I had been told by my mother many times of that day and of her deep regret for abandoning me in her despair. I remember her frequently telling me how competent I was as a young child. How after finally getting out of bed around 3 p.m., she found me—eighteen months old at the time—on the kitchen floor making my own sandwich. I would tell her in response how tragic that was, how out of necessity I learned to take care of myself or die. In fact my first sentence I put together around the same age was, "I want to do it all by myself!" I would learn time and again of how much my mother's early neglect shaped me. I would keep returning to my traumatized inner child for the rest of my life, bringing her new insights and new modalities to help her ultimately feel safe and loved.

As the feelings of unconditional love from my awakening began to fade, I decided to pursue a radically different professional direction, which began with leaving the publishing industry. At the time, I thought this departure would be permanent. I began to study how stress impacts the human system; I wanted to find a non-spiritual, biomedical explanation for what I had witnessed at work, as well as understand through a grounded, more scientific lens what I had directly experienced.

During a chance encounter at a small organic grocer, I met a young woman with a child my son's age. We chatted while shopping and she asked me if I knew about the magazine *Joyful Child* put out by Dr. Jenkins; we were both seeking to bring new, enlightened understanding to our role as mothers. Having not heard of Dr. Jenkins' work before, I quickly bought the latest issue of *Joyful Child*. Upon reading it, I realized that her work, her perspective on parenting, mirrored my early education at Forsyth School. I felt I had found the next step along my path.

Months later, I began training with Dr. Jenkins to be a parent educator, sharing with expectant mothers and young parents her principles, which were almost precise reflections of not only my new awareness, but also my earliest education. Dr. Jenkins' friend and colleague, Joseph Chilton Pearce, author of *The Magical Child, The Crack in the Cosmic Egg*, and many other groundbreaking books, had suggested to her that we check out the work of the HeartMath Institute. So I flew out to Boulder Creek, California, to attend a parenting seminar there that contextualized their research and the techniques they had developed for parents. I had found home. At least, that's what I thought at the time.

What I learned at HeartMath was in essence what I had learned at Forsyth, the only difference being HeartMath's scientific research on how what we feel affects the heart's rhythm—and frankly just about everything else, like the quality of our capacity to think, our biochemistry, our sense of fulfillment, and our resilience. I soon became certified to train others on their system and began conducting seminars in the greater St. Louis area, most often at the Unity Church that had housed Forsyth School twenty-five years earlier.

While teaching, I found that HeartMath's peer-reviewed scientific research on the role the heart and emotion plays in the human system was the most accessible way I could inform those not on a spiritual path, per se, to bring healing and greater emotional self-regulation to their daily lives. I also held private study groups at the church and found a deep sense of mission in sharing the work in a more intimate setting.

More importantly though was what I received. Each day in my own committed practice, I would remember how it felt when I awakened and I would choose to re-experience that feeling while focusing my attention in the heart, a technique HeartMath coined a *Heart Lock-In*. This is the same technique I used to create a ritual for my ancestors some thirty years later and the same technique I still use every day to continue to bring healing to my past traumas, while creating new neural circuitry grounded in love. Almost every time I locked into my heart, I remembered, as if my heart was leading me to all the places within myself that remained traumatized and stressed.

***

When my mother returned from the hospital after attempting to end her life, she returned with Joe. As a teenager, I used to tell my mother, after yet another violent outburst or moment of trauma, that she should expect nothing less; meeting a man in a mental hospital is likely the worse place to meet the love of your life, yet that is exactly what happened.

When I first met Joe, I was three years old and was immediately drawn to him, feeling an intense connection and love for a stranger. I wanted a man in our life, someone who would adore my mother and me and provide a much needed masculine presence.

Joe's hair was jet black, his skin smooth and olive, with a muscular physique that exuded strength and activity. Strikingly handsome, he had a youthful energy and he knew how to play. He was a man who stood in great contrast to my father whose hair was grey, his hairline receding, and his body not firm or muscular, instead flabby and neglected, and who would awkwardly try to play with me but struggled to do so. The only game my father and I ever played was cribbage, a heady card game not suitable for a child.

I loved Joe with all my heart. He would take his son, Jon, and me to the neighborhood pool and throw me high into the air. We would do gymnastics together at the local gym. He would sled with Jon and me on a snowy day, throwing snowballs, making snowmen. Yet there was intensity about him like a smoldering cauldron with the lid on so tight you sensed he could burst at any moment. Our first year with Joe was intoxicating. Then it all changed. Then he changed.

I don't remember what preceded his violence. I was four years old when he first burst. It was bedtime. Perhaps Jon was resisting going to bed. The sound of Joe's fist making contact with Jon's face is an unforgettable sound that brought me to the greatest fear I had yet known in the physical world. Jon was so sweet and gentle—a constant source of friendship for me. We were three months apart in age and, shortly after my mother returned from the hospital, she brought Jon to our home to live. Joe worked on the assembly line at GM and Jon's mother was unfit to care for him, so my mother, with her generous heart, provided Jon with much needed care. At the time, Joe didn't live with us; he lived in a modest low-income apartment and would visit but never stayed overnight.

Joe kept punching Jon. I kept screaming for it to stop. That's all I remember, but that night changed everything for me. I now felt deep mistrust of Joe, but also for my mother. *How could she bring this violence into our lives?*

As I got older, I began to withdraw. Joe's presence was something I held in deep contempt. Following Joe's first violent outburst,

I decided to go it alone. While my mother's love was something I could still feel, I knew in my heart that in order to thrive I needed to be anywhere else. Living with consistent trauma is mystical in that your memory of it is blurry and without detail. But you remember how it felt. It felt totally unsafe, so I chose to become someone who could care for herself without assistance.

***

Laying there on the chiropractor's table, I flashed back to Joe beating Jon as I hid behind a black-and-white checkered sleeper sofa, its texture so rough that it seemed unfit to sit on, trying to protect myself from his unpredictable rage. I saw myself coming home from high school, sensing before I opened the door that something frightening was happening on the other side. Holes in the walls, broken elegant furniture from my mother's past, the latest evidence of another of Joe's alcohol-induced tirade.

As those flashbacks occurred, I meditated, radiating feelings of love back to myself, rearchitecting my nervous system as I did, reframing the emotion of those moments, reassuring myself as a young girl that I was loved and ultimately safe.

By consciously remembering my past traumas, with the tools I had learned, some of which I developed myself, I could make sense of it all through a trauma-informed lens. I was working backwards in time, harnessing the energy of love through daily practice, collaborating with other healing practitioners like my network chiropractor, to bring as much conscious awareness as I could generate to continue to heal myself from my childhood trauma.

And as I continued to unpack it all, I realized too that my first marriage had ended before it started, when the most traumatic event of my young adult life occurred, altering the course of my life and my love life forever.

Chapter 10. Love and Marriage

"Well, Michael, if my daughter doesn't go out with you, I certainly will. You sound terrific!"

I rolled my eyes as I listened to my mother flirt with a man who had been earnestly calling me for over a month to go out on a date. I had motioned to her when the phone rang that if it was Michael calling, I wasn't home. I couldn't reconcile the age difference; I was twenty, Michael twenty-seven. That gap felt wide and scary. It didn't feel right.

After my mom hung up the phone, she counseled, "You've spent a great deal of time talking with him on the phone this past month. You say he's smart and interesting to talk to. Go out with him once and if you don't like him, don't do it again. And who knows? Maybe he'll have a friend you like."

Her counsel seemed reasonable so, in that moment, I decided if he called again I would say yes—on the condition that we double date with the people who were responsible for connecting us.

I was sitting quietly, reading in the messy apartment of my flamboyant friend, Char, as I waited for her daughter to wake from a nap. I was immediately drawn to Char when we met at the Midway Motor Lodge. Char looked like her name. She dressed in clothes just a size too tight, purposely revealing her buxom figure. She had no filter, was larger than life, and in some ways reminded me of my dear mother. It was the summer before my junior year in college and she trained me to be a waitress at the hotel that catered to business travelers. I wanted to earn money for the freedom that cash provided.

On this day, I was babysitting Char's daughter when I heard an aggressive knock on the door. Char and her live-in boyfriend, Roger, dealt in cocaine and I had no interest in answering the knock. I trusted that if I ignored the knocking, it would stop.

But it didn't. Frustrated that time hadn't dissuaded the knocker, I reluctantly got up out of my chair to see through the peephole who was so committed to knocking. As I peered, I saw a handsome man with large, thick-rimmed glasses, carrying a houseplant in his hands. I assumed he was from a floral delivery service and opened the door a crack. "Hi, can I help you?" The man explained he was there to give presents to Char and her daughter, who shared a birthday that weekend. The plant in his hands was for Char and a gift-wrapped puzzle was for her three-year-old child, Lauren, who was taking a nap. I was barely dressed in a long Oxford men's shirt, and curtly thanked him for the gifts, letting him know I would promptly give them to Char when she returned. We made a few minutes of small talk as I kept the door ajar, not inviting him to enter. As he left I felt nothing and didn't think much about the encounter. I certainly didn't think that I had just met the man who three years later would be my husband.

A few days later, Char asked me if she could give my phone number to the man bearing gifts. Without hesitation I told her no. Char gave Michael my number anyway and days later I was fielding his calls. Similar to the knocking that persisted, Michael continued to call to ask me out and I consistently told him no—until my mother counseled me to give it a go.

"Okay, Mike, sure. Saturday night works for me, but I'd like us to go out with Roger and Char." Looking back on it now, I think it's hysterical that I found safety in my chaperones, Roger and Char, two drug-dealing, hard-living adults who were a decade older than me. Roger was Michael's best friend from childhood and, while they had taken divergent paths, their sincere love for each other was palpable.

We ate dinner at a local café and then ventured out to a bar for a drink. I was twenty, though I looked more like fifteen, and I thought there was no way in hell I was going to convince the bouncer I was of drinking age. The line was long, the bar packed, and as we approached the bouncer, Char diverted his attention with her larger-than-life demeanor and large bosoms while Mike pushed me through, encouraging me to make a run for it. Drinks procured, we found a table. The atmosphere was smoky and loud—not conducive to meaningful conversation and getting acquainted.

Soon after we sat down, Char and Roger started arguing about something petty and Mike and I looked at each other, knowingly, with the intent to exit. A few minutes later, we said our goodbyes to them; they didn't seem to care, they were focused on their argument. We then ventured into the parking lot where we talked for a while and then he kissed me. It was the most passionate, meaningful kiss of my lifetime. I felt so alive. He then asked me to go boating with him the following day on Lake Carlyle. Without any hesitation, I said yes.

Our day on the lake was joyful. I felt so grown up as I sunned on the speedboat with Michael's friends, who were smart, successful, and easy in their connection. I listened intently as Mike's friend, Leo, regaled us with stories about the successful advertising firm he owned. As I confidently did a front flip off the edge of the boat, Michael greeted me in the water. As he held me there, I felt a complete peace in the presence of a man—a feeling I had never known before.

We spent the rest of the summer together. I essentially moved into the home that he shared with a few friends. His home was my safe haven and I felt like I had found the love of my life. We were together for the next twenty-five years.

A dear friend had once said that the end is always in the beginning, and for Michael and me, that was true. In my early twenties, my wounded inner child was driving me to create an adult life. Thus my choice of husband was, in many ways, a choice made to reconcile my childhood wounds. Michael had movie star good looks, curly black hair, inquisitive eyes, and a magazine-worthy physique. His intellect, his drive, his interest in the mystical experience, and his passionate love for me was an elixir I had never known.

I was heartbroken come fall, when I needed to return to college at the University of Missouri. Michael helped me move in to my new apartment that I shared with three dear friends. Our apartment was spacious: three bedrooms, two baths, a good-sized kitchen, a dining and living room—not a typical college apartment. My father supported me completely in college, paying for this rather opulent apartment, my tuition, and my car; in addition to $500 a month in spending money.

During our glorious, move-in weekend, Michael helped me unpack, studied *The Wall Street Journal*, then made my roommates and me homemade banana pancakes. We stayed up late talking intensely about everything and had glorious sex. The last afternoon, we sunned and swam in the apartment complex pool. As Michael took off his shirt, I could see my peers watching with attention. I felt a swooning love for him. His age, his career as a financial planner, his gorgeous face and physique filled me with a sense of pride. He was *my boyfriend*.

After he left to travel back home to St. Louis, I told my roommates that Michael and I would marry one day. I kidded them that if it turned out to not be true, they had my permission to give me endless shit about it. But if I was right, wasn't it amazing that I already knew?

Our time apart that semester was excruciating. Each time he would visit me or I would drive home to see him, our parting was intensely emotional. We would keep hugging and kissing as we said another goodbye and I would cry like a child. As I drove back to campus after one particular visit, I knew that this would be my last semester there. I transferred to a sister campus in St. Louis. I would lose a few credits, but I didn't care; the only thing that mattered to me was being with Michael.

I returned to St. Louis for Christmas and immediately moved in with him. Shortly after, we moved out of the house he was renting with friends and found a place of our own. Our apartment was tiny: a small galley kitchen too narrow for more than one person, a living room that could accommodate a small sofa and a couple of chairs, and our bedroom. Even simple everyday acts like going to the grocery store with Michael felt sacred.

My new school was going well too. I found my tribe at my new college and began training for competitive public speaking and debate. I started traveling across the country to compete. My best event was impromptu speaking in which I drew a topic from a bowl and then had less than a minute to craft a ten-minute speech. Michael would often travel with me to tournaments where he contributed to our efforts by being a lay judge. Each tournament had judges that were just everyday people, so Michael volunteered for the role so he could be by my side. A few events were televised on local cable access, including my debate against Oxford as well as a team that came from Soviet Russia. Boy, those Russians could drink!

College was easy, my grades were strong, and I felt fully alive, safe, and seen in my relationship. I was enthusiastically hopeful about my future. Michael and I got engaged, something I wanted with all my heart.

Then it all changed.

***

I parked my car in the back of our brownstone apartment building, as I had done day after a day after school and now, work. I loved coming home after a successful day in the field selling for Prentice Hall. After climbing the rickety fire escape stairs to reach the backdoor of my small apartment, I panicked. The doorknob was missing. Only a hole where it had resided remained.

I kicked the door open, briefcase in hand, stormed into the back hall, and ran down the short hallway, noticing that the walls were bare, no photographs or framed posters remained. "What the fuck?" I said out loud to myself. All the furniture, the knick-knacks we bought to fill our small space had disappeared. I thought we had been robbed. I frantically ran down the steps, heading to the front entrance of our building.

And there, cast carelessly on the street, were all of our belongings. Intimidating men, who looked like professional linebackers, were hurling our furniture and anything else they could scavenge into the back of their pickup truck. As soon as they saw me running out the front door, they sped away as I chased them, yelling at them to return my things. My heart was racing and I was screaming for help. But they were gone.

As I wept on the side of the road, trying to pick up the few things that had been left behind, the reality of what was happening hit me like a freight train. We had been evicted.

Even now, I do not remember anything that happened next. In my memory, all I can recall is where we lived next. I have no memory of where we slept that night. Perhaps my father bailed us out, though it seems unlikely given he was in deep trouble financially himself. Speculative real estate investments turned insolvent were draining him of cash and influence. My mother certainly had no resources to provide, she barely had enough money for food. And God knows there was no way Michael confided in his family for help. My inability to remember this still is a powerful reminder of how traumatic this day was in my young life. All I remember is the conscious choice I made after this frightening day to forgive and unconditionally love my fiancé despite him not paying our rent for months and not telling me about it. But what I failed to do was actually process the trauma. I bypassed my authentic feelings—my rage, my fear, my mistrust—and shifted immediately to forgiveness. In so doing, this day would be the end of my marriage before it had begun. I was being given a sign that my future with Michael would be fraught with instability, yet I didn't see that. I loved him so deeply. I knew how sorry he was that he hadn't paid rent, and I chose to ignore the signs and proceed as if nothing had happened.

As the years went on, I began to realize how pivotal this day was for me and for my marriage. I held an unconscious mistrust of Michael because of his deceit about his financial health as we began our married lives together. Unsurprisingly, this would not be the last time he would lie or make financial decisions that would cause me harm.

Had I processed this trauma, perhaps I could have found a path back to seeing my husband as someone I could count on, who had my back, who I could fully let my trauma-informed guard down around. Instead this moment fueled my fire to be fiercely independent, to rely on no one else, just as my traumatic childhood had. The fire was also fueling my belief that my corporate ascension and productivity could keep me safe from harm. But more importantly, it created an unconscious emotional distance between Michael and me that would widen as the years went on. Intimacy with someone you don't trust is impossible. My traumatized inner child disliked Michael because he was yet another person I deeply loved who had shattered my trust.

Like a mirror of my childhood, our twenty-two years of marriage would go on to be both a great love and a great source of instability and pain. The polarity that colored our union reminded me of the opening of Charles Dickens' novel, *A Tale of Two Cities*,

> It was the best of times, it was the worst of times, it was the age of wisdom, it was the age of foolishness, it was the epoch of belief, it was the epoch of incredulity, it was the season of light, it was the season of darkness, it was the spring of hope, it was the winter of despair.

Chapter 11. Heading West

As a young girl, I had a recurring dream. A long wooden dock led to an expansive lake. I would walk slowly to the edge of the dock and dive in. In the depths of the lake, there was a mystical world filled with people in monk-like, black robes, hoods draped over their heads, and they would float about, in almost formless shapes, with a light illuminating from their hearts. I would observe these people with reservation, always finding some kind of physical barrier to hide behind as I watched them float about. No words were spoken, just me hiding in guarded observation. And I would then wake up. I had this dream countless times as a child. The dream had me always curious, not frightened. *Who were these people? Why did I continue to visit them in my dreams night after night?*

Post awakening, after I learned about the HeartMath Institute and became certified to train others on their system, I flew to California several times a year to deepen my connection to their work.

During winters in the Santa Cruz Mountains back then, rain was an almost constant. I ran briskly across a meadow with my short London Fog raincoat as my only protection from the pouring rain. I didn't want to be late for the workshop that was beginning. With the black raincoat hood draped over my head, I suddenly remembered my dream. I felt immediately a knowing inside that this group of people, dedicated to teaching people about the power of the heart, were the figures I saw repeatedly in my dream. I giggled to myself as I thought about the dock that I would dive off in the dream—the founder of HeartMath, the mystic who led these people, who developed this transformative system, was named *Doc* Childre. Dock. In that moment, I knew deep in my heart that I needed to move to Boulder Creek and join them full time.

I had a clear heart directive, and I also had a husband and a four-year-old son.

Over the years of our early marriage and new parenthood, the divide had deepened between Michael and me. Yet there were moments of deep joy and connection too. While he accepted the radical change that I had now embodied, we struggled to connect, as if we were literally on different wavelengths. I met him with vast unconditional love, yet wondered if our union was healthy or strong enough to hold the change within me and the changes I knew I needed to make.

We lived in a beautiful urban neighborhood with well-manicured lawns, large oaks with their branches bending toward the street, homes built mostly in the 1930s, meticulously maintained. A couple of years post-awakening, Michael and I had gone across the street to a cocktail party hosted by our neighbors who were not really friends, more like friendly acquaintances. I was given a martini in an exquisite crystal glass and found myself in conversation with a group of women focused on talking in great detail about the new, raw silk, handmade drapes. I think even before my awakening I would have had no interest in this conversation, but on this day it served as a glaring symbol of the disconnect between the life I had led prior to my awakening and the person I now was.

I graciously abandoned the conversation, found Michael talking to the men in another room, and motioned for him to come toward me. "I simply can't do this anymore. It doesn't resonate with what I value. I know I need to move to Boulder Creek and work at HeartMath."

Clear heart directives often feel abrupt to others. When we are able to truly get to the heart of something, it has an uncompromising quality about it. I wasn't sure if I was going to be moving to Boulder Creek with just my son or whether Michael would join me, but I held no fear. I trusted that, however this was to unfold, it would unfold, as it should. Michael's love for me had a wide generosity about it. And even though he had the habit of emotional dysregulation, losing his temper, saying things so mean spirited it could take my breath away, he also had a vast capacity to be loving and to love. Similar to my mother, yes?

After my truth telling at the cocktail party, Michael and I had many deep talks. In vulnerable moments, he admitted that his work wasn't meeting his heart but he feared radical change. Who wouldn't? Selling our home, selling his investment advisory practice to his partner, so I could go to work at HeartMath for literally twelve dollars an hour was what I was asking of him. It was a *big* ask. Yet I was crystal clear that moving to a small town in the Santa Cruz Mountains, with fewer than 6,000 residents, where meth labs were often adjacent to monasteries, was where I needed to be to align with my heart and my mission.

So in the summer of 1999, five years after my awakening, we packed our blue Volvo station wagon, said a tearful goodbye to family and friends, and began our journey to California. I held great hope that this move would provide a fresh start for my marriage while giving me an incredible opportunity to be of service with my renewed understanding and Divine access.

We had purchased a sweet house just a few blocks from HeartMath's business office, surrounded by redwood forest and just a short walk to the San Lorenzo River that flowed on the outskirts of town. The home had a large deck in the back with two mature redwoods growing through the center encircled by a redwood bench. Expansive windows allowed sunlight to stream through to the living room where a large fireplace, built with local river rock, served as a focal point for the nurturing space. In the front of the house was a separate large room, at least 600 square feet, with its own entrance and full bath that we intended for my mother and Joe to live in. The idea of living far away from my mother was ripe with conflicted emotions. Part of me longed for distance, to physically separate myself from her extremes. Yet a larger part of me wanted to care for her—to give her a chance to live in new surroundings, full of magic, that perhaps could serve as a healing new start. The idea of rarely seeing my mother simply didn't feel right. So we proceeded with the latter plan, investing money to get their house ready for sale. Once sold, they would move into the space that seemed ideally suited for them to live while also providing some privacy.

When I first told her my plans, not mentioning the thought of bringing her and Joe along, she quickly responded, "Yes! Go. I have lived in many places across the world and frankly I don't even understand why I'm still here in St. Louis. I don't want you to feel held back by me, go live your life, knowing always how much I love you." Yet she also cautioned me, saying, "You know, honey, people don't really change because of a workshop. They change only through their own sincere discovery. In fact, the discovery method is the only one that counts."

When I asked my mother if she wanted to move with us, she enthusiastically agreed, not hesitating for a moment in her response. I sensed she couldn't bear living without her only grandchild and me.

All the details of preparing for the move—Michael's exit from his company, buying and selling our homes—happened with ease. Renovating my mother's home to sell it was going to take some time, so we knew they wouldn't be joining us for at least six months. It felt as if what was ahead was going to be full of aligned magic. Michael and I agreed that for the first year we would live off the proceeds from the sale of his business. My minimum wage job with HeartMath was certainly not going to be enough to live on. We also agreed that, during that year, Michael would care for Connor and engage in deep inquiry to plan for his next career step. I had no doubt about the rightness of this plan. I trusted that Michael would take beautiful care of Connor and figure out in time what his next step would be.

My role at HeartMath was as lead trainer for business audiences, as well as finding new corporate clients. The pull to come there to work lived in my heart, was foreshadowed in my childhood dreams, but was also personified in the love and connection I felt for HeartMath's CEO, Bruce Cryer. At the time, I did not feel romantic love for Bruce, rather a deep kinship. Some years before, Bruce had come to work with me in St. Louis. We sat on my screened-in porch talking deeply about the HeartMath mission. He told me on that trip that I had an open invitation to come and work there as an employee. And while it took a few years to come together, I remembered vividly what happened that evening as I put my toddler Connor to sleep. Connor was an unusual child. He was wise beyond his years and would often utter such profundity, remembering with great detail previous lives and referring to them, sharing wisdom about the purpose of living, talking often about how we are made of light. That night, as we said our prayers before putting him to sleep, Connor exclaimed, "And God bless Bruce Cryer, who used to be my father." Connor recognized that Bruce was part of our soul family too.

I woke up early for my first day of work with deep excitement. I was thrilled to be representing HeartMath, looking forward to the retreats that Bruce and I would be leading for business audiences. I felt such rightness about it all.

Then, two hours into my first day, I felt like I had made a colossal mistake. When I arrived, I was met by one of the staff whose task was to give me an orientation, yet spent most of our time "training" me on how to fill out a time sheet. *For God's sake*, I thought, *time sheets are rather self-explanatory.* There was something amateurish about the interaction; I did not feel seen. People treated me as if I were some naïve girl with no wisdom to offer, much less someone who had had a high-performing business career or a life-changing awakening. They did not hold any curiosity about me. There was no inquiry about who I was or what my life experience had been, nor did most seem to have any interest in becoming more emotionally connected. People there who I hadn't known well prior to the move felt insincere. I felt a substantial disconnect with the work they represented and the people themselves. And I quickly learned that first day, mostly through observation and intuition, that the founding staff lacked freedom. They all lived and worked communally. What they ate, their housing, who they partnered with, how they spent their time, was not determined by themselves. It was determined by Doc.

I wanted nothing to do with this. I felt like I had agreed to work for some kind of benevolent cult. And while I felt deep gratitude for the tools and research they developed, for I knew firsthand how transformational their tools were to transmute stress and connect more deeply to the intelligence of the heart, I felt a deep disconnect between those tools and the staff themselves. After lunch, I shared with Bruce that I had no interest in participating in any of it other than leading people in programs and finding new clients. And while I hadn't been asked to join their evening ritual of "camp" with Doc, where they continued to work late into the night, deepening their relationship with their own hearts, I wanted no part in it. I immediately and suddenly, on my first day, felt a mistrust of the place and particularly a mistrust of Doc himself. Even my four year old shared my mistrust. One day I took him with me to the "land" which housed the research center, the retreat facility and housing for staff. There, standing outside one of the buildings, was

Doc. I wanted to buy a new hammock for the house and thought maybe he could suggest a place. As I got within 100 yards of Doc, Connor looked up at me and said, "Mom, I will wait here." He had no interest in getting any closer to him.

During my first week, I called my mother from my desk, confiding in her that I felt like I had made a huge mistake. "Oh, love," she wisely responded, "what you're not seeing is how far these people have come from where they started." Hearing that, I was able to access more compassion for them. But it still didn't feel right.

During my first months there, I remained disciplined in my practice. Heart-centered meditations were still part of my daily routine and facilitating the HeartMath experience for others helped, for a time, to keep my awareness deep and wide in my heart. I enjoyed leading programs, traveling across the country to bring HeartMath tools to the business community. Yet my time in the office felt rigid. When I was there, there was a tightness, a lack of flexibility in my daily interactions. The freedom I had felt in my own system, catalyzed by my awakening, began to feel squeezed. I felt as if I couldn't be myself. That I had to somehow adapt to this restrictive energy that permeated the office setting.

One morning, before heading off to lead a training at Cisco Systems, I shared an analogy with Bruce. Having recently watched the film *Elizabeth*, I saw parallels in my experience. In her young life before becoming queen, she was a free spirit. In an evocative scene capturing her life before, she was free to express herself, moving with abandon, twirling, arms out wide, in an expansive green field without a care in the world. Her heart was open and she was fully herself. Then the movie concludes by capturing the burden of duty, her inability to be open, free, and connected. The very last scene zooms in on her whitened, powdered faced. She is wearing restrictive clothing to suit her role, with white lace tight around her neck. She looks without life. "I feel like her," I told Bruce, "I feel so choked off from expansion. I don't feel seen. I feel as if my connection to higher awareness is now interrupted as if there is a knot choking off my access." It was clear in that moment that Bruce didn't want to acknowledge my truth. Or at least he didn't seem to understand how the energetics of the place was impacting my sense of myself and my connection to the Divine.

As I entered the Cisco office complex, following their rather rigid rules of entrance, I was given my visitor badge and escorted to the conference room, where I was to train a group of rogue customer service representatives who were being forced to attend my training due to rude interactions with customers, which had been flagged by their automated customer feedback system. As my escort and I approached the room, walking down the long, narrow hall, I saw that each conference room was named. My room, I saw as we arrived, was marked by a plaque, which in bold-faced type, read: "Queen Elizabeth."

Spirit had affirmed my feelings with a bit of welcome humor. I entered the Queen Elizabeth Room and began setting up, connecting to their AV system, troubleshooting to ensure that my PowerPoint presentation would connect to the projector as well as the HeartMath software that I would demonstrate. HeartMath had developed a technology to see your heart rhythms in real time. When you are connected to heart-centered feelings of love and appreciation, as you focus your attention in your heart by directing your breath there, your rhythm changes. The stronger you are able to connect to the heart, the more coherent your rhythm becomes. Ideally, becoming a smooth, sine, wave-like shape, like gentle, even hills that correlate with the even activation of your sympathetic and parasympathetic nervous systems.

As my audience came straggling in, I could feel their resistance; a fuck-you attitude was immediately palpable and I knew I had my work cut out for me. They were mandated, aggressive, and reluctant. I acknowledged to myself that my physical appearance didn't exude credibility. While I was now thirty-two, people often thought I was in my early twenties; I had a pixie haircut, a petite frame, and a youthful exuberance that didn't scream credible presenter. I got carded anytime I went to buy wine. I knew that I would need to spend more time than I typically did on the science for these people, building the credibility of this approach by spending more time reviewing the peer-reviewed literature, helping this group understand the real impact that the stress response has on the human system.

I began, sharing with them that when we are stressed, frustrated, and angry, the rhythm of our hearts is chaotic and the biochemistry of those moments impacts our health over time, decreasing immune function and inhibiting cognitive function. As I shared it all with them, they became a bit more responsive. Yet the general energetic feedback I was getting from my audience was still, "I'm not buying what you're selling. Shut the fuck up!" One of the participants stood out to me in particular. He was radiating anger and had a menacing presence—large and muscular, like a professional linebacker. He was clearly trying to intimidate with his angry gaze and physical size.

Undeterred, I continued demonstrating the software, getting one volunteer to come forward so all could see the real-time difference in her heart rhythm when recalling a moment of great stress contrasted with recalling a moment when she felt love or gratitude. Feeling a bit of a shift in my audience, it was now time to take them through a heart-centered meditation: a Heart Lock-In. Their resistance was still perceptible as I dimmed the lights and led them through the process. I focused my attention on the linebacker in particular, sensing he was the tacit leader of this group. Feeling a bit of over care in my system, wondering how this was all landing for them, I was thankful that this transformative technique was easy to teach and easy to learn. I directed them to focus their attention in their hearts, as if they were breathing through their hearts, guiding them to find an easeful rhythm of breath. Then I asked them to think of a moment in time when they felt deep appreciation, love for someone or something, moving beyond the mental image of that moment to the feeling itself and directing them to re-experience that feeling as they continued to breathe through their hearts. Once the positive emotion was activated, I then was silent, just allowing them the time and space to soak in that positive emotional state. A few minutes passed and I instructed them to open their eyes as I gradually turned the lights back on. I believed, knew, and had witnessed many times the transformative power of this technique, but with this group, who knew how it would land?

They opened their eyes and I looked at them, taking them in. Then, to my shock and delight, the linebacker stood up, extending his arms high above his head with his face shining up towards the ceiling, and exclaimed, "This is exactly what I need!" After his enthusiastic endorsement, the rest of the day my audience was deeply engaged, asked lots of vulnerable questions, and I felt so good inside knowing I had brought new tools to them that, if practiced, could change their lives.

Given the synchronicity of working in the Queen Elizabeth Room that day, I was determined, as I repacked my equipment and said a kind goodbye to my converted audience, to reclaim my power, my access, my sense of internal freedom, and not to try to fit in with the group of people back at work that held little resonance for me.

Returning to the office, I focused on my connections with those I felt good around—those who had recently come to work there, like me, from elsewhere. Ed, an executive coach with a huge heart and a deep belly laugh, was leading the sales team. Another, Jim, had worked on Wall Street and had been taught HeartMath by the actress Linda Gray at a Manhattan cocktail party, and similar to me, Jim had left an externally abundant life, a glamorous Manhattan apartment, to move to a studio cabin in the redwoods that looked like a scene from the movie *Deliverance*. We understood each other.

Perhaps because we had lived out in the world our whole adult lives, in stark contrast to those we worked with, who had joined Doc decades before, becoming renunciates, giving all their money and freedom to Doc and the mission. Jim and I would have long, deep, talks about the strangeness of our daily work lives, how it lacked joy, freedom, a sense of aliveness, and how cut off the HeartMath staff seemed to be from everyday reality.

One afternoon after lunch, Jim and I sat on the concrete patio, which years before had been a community pool, and fantasized about having Big Wheel races across the concrete. A simple, child-like act of rebellion to reconnect to freedom, expansion, and expression. We laughed a lot; our laughter helped to release the tension we both felt about working there.

Each day the kitchen staff would prepare lunch for everyone. The food was usually delicious, simple in preparation, and made with deep care. On this fateful day, as I stood in line with my plate in hand waiting to get my lunch, I noticed that hamburgers were being served. Then I noticed that no ketchup was out on the counter. For me hamburgers and ketchup go together. "Phil, where's the ketchup?" I asked the head chef.

"Regan, Sara and Doc don't want us to have the added sugar today," he quickly responded. I felt this surge of energy climb within and I yelled loud enough so all could hear, "I am in charge of my own condiments! No one is going to tell me what I can eat or how I can eat it!" I then stormed to the pantry, grabbed a bottle of ketchup, and generously poured it all over my hamburger.

And that moment, less than a year after I had started, was the end of my HeartMath career.

Even though my sense of aloneness at work—with the exception of Ed and Jim—was a constant, my connection to Bruce had deepened. We spent a great deal of time together co-facilitating programs, and a deeper relationship began to bloom. I had fallen in love with him. I knew I needed to find a graceful way out. No good would come from this ecstatic connection, that much I knew. I had no interest in having an affair, not that Bruce was giving me any indication he wanted to have one, yet my feelings were strong and almost felt out of my control. I thought to myself, *What the hell am I going to do*? Here I had thought this work was my life's mission, yet the circumstances I now found myself in felt so misaligned and unsustainable.

Doc had taken an interest in Michael and invited him to "camp" each week with a collection of other men with whom he was building a deep, connected relationship. I mistrusted Doc's intention, with no empirical evidence. Just a feeling.

One night, Michael returned from camp and told me he wanted to give a great deal of money to HeartMath. In fact, he said he had this impulse to give them everything we had. Months prior, some of the founders had visited our home and asked us if we would be willing to take out a loan against our mortgage to provide them needed funds. Privately, I told Michael that in no way did I feel right about any of this. I felt like he was being manipulated.

Against my counsel and explicit desire, Michael chose to give the organization $50,000, a sizable chunk of the $300,000 we had gained selling Michael's business, which was the only financial resource we had to support our family. Michael's choice took away my voice in our decisions about the funds. And while part of me understood that he felt he had that right, for it was the money from the sale of the business he had built, it still felt wrong. It wasn't a partnership if he could make choices about our finances without my consent and support—even against it.

Michael had also started a business with a friend called Kidocracy. It was the wild Internet business days, when it somehow no longer mattered if you had a business model as long as you had users. I intuitively knew it wasn't going to amount to anything and found a way to kindly tell Michael that I didn't think it was a wise investment of our limited resources. But he didn't listen. I watched him spend our money on renting an office and furnishing it, sensing that our lives were unraveling at a quick clip.

At this time, I prayed a lot for clarity and guidance. And then the Divine intervened and provided me with a graceful but complicated exit.

My mother and Joe came to visit around this time and the visit broke my heart. Looking back on it now, I can access more compassion for my mother; I know my moving away with her only grandson had further broken her. Even though we had committed to eventually having them live with us and share in the new life we were building, the foundation for that life was crumbling and perhaps she sensed that. Whatever the reason, on that visit she was cruel in unregulated outbursts that have no clear detail in my memory now. My mother, as she aged with so much unresolved trauma within her, had a way of speaking where you felt like she was ripping your skin off. She never spoke a word that wasn't true, yet there was a brutality in how it came out. And while I don't remember what she said, I remember how I felt, which was immensely protective of my young son and myself.

What I do remember was her treating me with such brutality, I put down an uncompromising boundary. We had gone to a nearby town to have dinner at a delicious Italian restaurant with outdoor seating. Redwood trees surrounded us and there were thoughtful touches for children, toys to play with, and a sandbox—fun distractions for my four-year-old son. As we were served our dinner, my mother began unloading on me. I wish I could remember what she had said, but I cannot. I glanced towards my son as she screamed at me and watched as a tear fell down his cheek. In that moment, I was able to access my heart, while telling her firmly and lovingly what my truth was. I told her, gently, firmly, that she was no longer welcome to move in with us and that if she didn't figure out how to shift out of whatever was consuming her, that this would be her last visit.

In the few days left of their visit, she was able to shift and be the magnetically loving person she could be, yet even still, I was done. I wanted to protect my child; her presence simply wasn't safe.

Our second Christmas in our home in the redwoods had a sweet feeling about it. And while Michael and I had conflict, mostly over money, our days were still filled with an expansive love, particularly for Connor, who had just turned five. I had inner conflict of course, due to my feelings for Bruce, but I was committed not to act on those, sensing that somehow it was all going to shift and change. My dear friend, Marcy, the one who had hired me years before to work at Prentice Hall, had moved to the Bay Area. Having her thirty miles or so from me was deeply comforting. Michael, Connor, and I met her and her new husband for brunch along with a group of interesting friends they had met, but for days I hadn't felt well. I was nauseous, but attributed feeling unwell to the rich food and drink that predominated that time of year. As I sat at the long table, hardly able to eat the delicious brunch, that still, quiet voice within said, "Go to the nearby Walgreens and buy a pregnancy test."

I was shocked. Until that moment it had never occurred to me that why I felt unwell could be pregnancy related. I whispered to Michael, "I'll be back in a few minutes. I'm going to buy a pregnancy test." He looked at me with great surprise and love. I then walked out of the café, walked a few blocks, feeling like I might throw up at any time, purchased the test, and asked the clerk if I could use their bathroom. As I sat on the commode, reading the signs about the requirement to wash hands, rules about workplace safety, staring at the peeling paint in this bathroom that desperately needed a deep cleaning, I pulled the white stick out from under me, and it revealed that I was indeed pregnant.

A few weeks before, at a local shop showcasing artists from the community, I had purchased an inexpensive but beautiful painting. It was an abstract, large angel with its wings fully expressed. Within its expansive shape was a smaller angel. I guess my higher self knew I was holding a new life inside of me, though I wasn't conscious of it yet. This pregnancy was a complete surprise, so unlike the moment we had conceived Connor a few days after my awakening. I had grown grateful that my psychic gifts didn't always reveal. Life is more interesting and more impactful, particularly when the major events reveal themselves naturally, without premonition. My growing child was a surprise to me.

As my belly grew, I continued to travel, leading HeartMath programs across the country. I could see in the eyes of my audience feelings of trepidation about my size—people would often ask me if I was carrying twins. I would always need to reassure my audiences that my due date was long away, delivery not imminent, as I munched on saltines, drinking ginger ale during breaks to try to curb my ever-present nausea. The pregnancy provided a bit of a reset for Michael and me. We tried to put our differences aside to focus on our growing family. As soon as I learned I was pregnant, I had shared the news with Bruce and that announcement put an abrupt end to any feelings that had been present. I resigned from HeartMath a few months before my due date of August 17, 2000. I wanted to spend the summer with Connor, soak up as much joy as I could with him, knowing that our lives would change when the new baby arrived.

My last day at HeartMath was heartbreaking. They didn't seem to care that I had come or that I was leaving. There was no outward expression of appreciation for my time there, or how I had represented HeartMath to business audiences across the country. As I walked out of the office for the last time, I ran into Bruce. He said only a curt goodbye, clearly busy with the demands of his day. My heart sank as I left that day. As I walked to my car, I prayed that life would somehow begin to make more sense, that somehow my growing family would find its way forward.

What I didn't know then, and know now, was that coming to California, and how my life would continue to unfold, would provide me ample opportunity for growth. That I would always be guided back to myself and to my prayer. I didn't know that in the decades that followed that I would become my own best teacher. I would learn that I did not need to follow someone else's innovation. While I could be informed by many, what I needed to do was create my own process within my own heart.

Yet it would be a complicated path, filled with tumult, pain, heartbreak, change, new relationships, unexpected people, and professional directions that, in the end, would lead to my liberation once more.

Chapter 12. Goodbye

Some thirty years after first meeting Michael, I took extra time in the morning, putting deliberate care into my makeup, curling my hair, and choosing a summer dress comfortable for the heat but still feminine. I wanted to look my best for our goodbye. The day before, I had shopped for a gift and card that could help me express the vast, unconditional love that remained within me. We were meeting for lunch to say our farewells.

Seven years earlier, Michael had declared bankruptcy. Shortly after that, we had divorced. His decision to carelessly invest in real estate had caught up with him. I found it curious that the real estate investing was very similar to my father's decades before that had brought him to the brink of bankruptcy for the rest of his life. I am sure a therapist would marvel at the mirrored circumstance. Though I'm unclear of transactional details, whomever Michael had recruited to invest in these speculative real estate deals had enough cause to sue him for some kind of negligence. Faced with imminent litigation, he chose to protect himself as best he could, which was to declare insolvency. The years that followed were a true struggle for him. He liquidated his investment advisory company, selling it to a local firm. Throughout, he earnestly applied the tools he had learned from me, namely the techniques of HeartMath, to keep himself as emotionally regulated as he could during this fraught time. And he prayed, a lot. He formed different partnerships to provide impact investment consulting services to community foundations across the country, yet his efforts to generate income for himself yielded few results. He was running out of time. I marveled at his capacity to stay committed to meditation and prayer. And while he was no longer my husband, I was rooting for him.

Thankfully, he met a woman who had a very successful legal career and their love sustained him. He moved in with her and her three-year-old son. He had found a safe haven, yet was unable to find work. In times of struggle, we often choose to return home. After a number of conversations with his former business partner back in St. Louis, he was extended an offer to return to the investment advisory firm he had helped start some twenty-five years earlier. He was moving back home to begin another chapter, coming back to a bit of a hero's welcome, for many of the investment advisors he had mentored many years ago were still there.

Our children, now young adults, were conflicted about him moving out of state. While they hadn't lived with him for many years, his leaving was a loss to us all.

As I glanced at the various greeting cards, trying to find the right sentiment for our goodbye lunch, I saw one with two goldfish, swimming alone in their respective fishbowls, looking at one another. I picked it up off the shelf and began to cry. After the eviction, I had built a metaphorical wall to protect myself, never able to trust him again. But like a fishbowl, the wall was made of glass—fragile and capable of cracking, but still able to let love shine in and out. I was immediately reminded of the Pink Floyd song "Wish You Were Here."

Even after all the tumult that occurred in our marriage, there was a piece of me that wished he "were here"—in my life as my partner. I had struggled to fully accept him as he was, not as I wanted him to be. It is easy to acknowledge and love what looks like and feels like love, but it was deeply difficult for me to acknowledge the darkness and the trauma that the people central to my life represented. Unconditional acceptance is forgiveness with clear eyes about harm caused. We forgive not to make it okay, not to somehow justify the traumatizing choices of others, but to liberate ourselves from it. To say: what you did was so not okay that I choose not to be connected it to it anymore.

In order to liberate myself from it all, I had to actually acknowledge the truth of what I had experienced, surrender it back to love, and be released from it.

I finally see Michael in the distance, walking down a flight of concrete steps. Dressed in shorts and a tailored shirt, his hair salt and pepper, his skin tanned by his time exercising outdoors, he looked handsome, fit, and happy. He sprung down the steps and gave me a big hug. "Hi, Re." His calling me Re reflected our history, only those who knew me young knew to call me Re. I immediately teared up as I handed him his gift and card to carry as we walked to lunch. We each ordered a glass a wine and as we talked about the details of his move, I wanted to pivot the conversation.

"Please open your card." I sensed if I didn't interrupt, the conversation wouldn't lead to the depth I was seeking. He looked solemn as he read. I had intended to convey in the words what was true for me. One of our strengths was our capacity to communicate truth to each other. I told him how much I regretted our failure, how the loss of our union remained within me, how I took responsibility for what was mine. And I closed by telling him how I wanted nothing more for him than to have love, ease, and prosperity in his choices ahead. He looked up and said, "Thank you, Re." It was clear he didn't want to say anything more. He then opened his gift: a handmade glass heart, framed in gold, which I had bought from a local artist, Annie Glass. The heart was our symbol. We had learned in time how to access the power of the heart, as husband and wife; we had become deeply committed students of its teachings. I was comforted knowing that my awakening had helped teach us both something profound about its capacity to transform trauma. I hoped that in his new home in St. Louis, he would glance at the heart and be reminded of what we had learned together.

A common thread in my life had been leapfrogging over authentic feeling and launching myself into unconditional love. I would circumvent feeling the consequence of trauma by choosing unconditional love instead. And while unconditional love is the true destination, we can't heal by bypassing the truth of our experience. Just as I had done lying on the chiropractor's table, feeling the magnitude of the trauma of my mother's suicide attempt, I knew that the last mile within me was to *fully acknowledge* the pain of what I had experienced with Michael and feel into the parallels of who my mother and he both were and how their choices affected me. I also knew that my choices over time not having a disciplined daily practice to keep alive my awakened state had led to my part in our dissolution.

I know precisely when I had begun to abandon myself again. I now have great insight and compassion for myself. Even though I had had a spiritual education so young and a dramatic awakening, the magnitude of my trauma was bigger than I consciously understood. As I walked away from Michael, I paused and reflected on the moment. I felt deep love for myself and for Michael, too. I acknowledged to myself that I wouldn't want anything to be different. All of it was apparently necessary to bring me to who I was becoming.

Chapter 13. Adapt

Ian was just a year old when Michael sat me down with a stern look on his face and said, "Re, we are running out of money."

Living in the Santa Cruz Mountains was expensive. Michael had been reckless, spending money on his business ideas and giving to HeartMath as if he were some kind of wealthy patron. I didn't attend to our budget and, while I wasn't extravagant, I didn't hold in my awareness a need to be frugal. We had lived as if the $300,000 we had received from the sale of Michael's investment advisory practice to his partner was going to last forever. Well, it didn't.

A value I deeply held then, and still do today, is the vital importance of a mother staying home to care for her infant. Given the neglect I experienced so young, I was committed to deeply bonding with my baby. But with Michael's news, I knew I would need to find work. I was devastated. But instead of choosing to feel into my truth, instead of reflecting on all the options available, I charged ahead. And while Michael was going to form a new investment advisory firm, we both recognized it would take him years to earn enough to support the family. I needed to work.

It was in that moment—the moment when I could no longer stay home and tend to my children as I wanted to—that my marriage ended, though I wasn't fully conscious of it. All my inner resources were now focused on finding work in an industry I never thought I would return to. Having had only one career—in publishing—the only logical place to find work was back in the industry I knew. As I began to process it all, I did the math. Seven years had passed since I had left my publishing career, and while knowing it as well as I had provided a bit of confidence, I was unsure that I could find my way back to a job that could support the family. 2001 was a very different climate than 1994. Seven years without any relevant industry experience was a big gap. The Internet was forcing true change yet I had professionally excelled in the print world, not the digital world. Yet my renewed spirit from my awakening gave me some hope that with God's help I could find a way to somehow make it work.

"Do you know Jim Kelly? He and Ed Stanford are creating a new division at McGraw-Hill and they are looking for someone to manage the West." My friend and HeartMath coaching client, Rob, an executive with Pearson, a large education conglomerate, shared the news when I confided in him my need to find corporate work. I felt deep relief hearing about this opportunity. I knew Jim and Ed. I thought maybe I'd have a shot, given that Jim had been my vice-president for a short time at Prentice Hall, the year I had been the number one sales rep.

A few days later, as I waited on hold for Jim to come on the line, my stomach churned and I could feel my heart beating rapidly. I was desperate. I also had enough presence to pray for the highest good as I waited on the line. We had only a few thousand dollars left. My inner world was a mix of intense emotion as I waited for Jim to come on the line. Angry at Michael. Deeply sad at the thought of not being with my baby, Ian. Wanting nothing more than to have a healthy marriage where I felt secure and held. My breasts ached, filled with the milk that somehow I might need to figure out how to provide my baby while traveling all over the West.

I was overwhelmed, but I needed to stuff my grief deep inside and appear enthusiastic for Jim. "Hi, Jim, it's Regan Caruthers. I learned from Rob that you are looking for someone to drive sales in the West. I'd love to learn more, it sounds like an amazing opportunity." I learned years later that upon hearing me say, "It is Regan Caruthers," Jim had decided in that moment to hire me—if that was the reason I was calling. He flew out to interview me a few days after we briefly spoke. I can still vividly remember what I wore to the interview. I struggled to find something appropriate, given that I still had baby weight, and most of my professional clothes, which reflected a life I never thought I would live again, didn't fit. I found a green wool pencil skirt with the waist secured by a large diaper pin to give me an inch or so more room, a grey blazer, a turtleneck sweater, and black shoe boots. I was back in the corporate uniform.

Jim was quiet and kind. I hadn't known him well when we worked together years earlier, but I didn't like him very much, for no valid reason other than he represented an industry I had grown to dislike, given its patriarchal tendencies and how I was treated when I worked for its leadership.

Jim and I spoke for hours. His gentle, kind, yet strategic demeanor was easy to be with. I thought to myself, *If I have to go back to work doing something that feels like it's greatly opposed to my values, at least I will have a sweet boss.* As he described the role, I felt sincere excitement; this job would be different from anything I had done in the past. Publishing was needing to change, given the Internet. McGraw-Hill was trying to figure out how to pivot to digital, how to become more of a software company than a publisher of books. This role would call on presidents and provosts of universities with the intent of partnering at the institutional level, as opposed to working with faculty and convincing them to use print textbooks.

"Would you find it intimidating to call on university leaders?" Jim asked with a twinkle in his green piercing eyes. I think he knew my answer. I still exuded a charismatic confidence—a take-charge attitude. My choice of response to my life trauma, my I-can-do-it-all-by-myself attitude, was a perfect fit for a role that had never been done before. I responded to Jim's question by sharing a bit about my parents: how my mother had dated a king, how my father would have presidential candidates over for dinner.

"No, Jim. Given how I was raised, nothing really intimidates me."

A week or so later, Jim offered me the job. I was now the eLearning Director for McGraw-Hill, with on target earnings of over six figures, a company car, full benefits, and a 401(k). On the one hand, I was relieved because we needed to pay our mortgage and feed ourselves. On the other hand, I was desperately sad because I could no longer mother my baby or care for my older son on a fulltime basis.

After I interviewed with Jim, I began to look for childcare. I had a few leads from hanging around the organic café on the main street of my small mountain town. The owner's partner was a stay-at-home mom, and I trusted her. She parented consciously, exuded a stable and calm presence, and I prayed that she would be willing to help. Thankfully, Shanda said yes. As I drove the short drive to their property, my heart ached. Literally the last thing I wanted to do was to leave my baby with this kind stranger, yet I was grateful to have found a conscious, loving caretaker for my baby. Shanda would lead me a year later to Max, a renaissance man who played the saxophone, studied the Quran, had dreadlocks down to his ankles, and exuded a tender, loving intelligence. Max would help care for my children for the next nine years.

I still vividly remember my first successful meeting in my new job. I flew to Long Beach, California, to meet with the head of academic technology for the California State University system. This person was central to any academic innovation in the state and, if I could inspire him to want to partner with me, I could make a big, strategic impact in my new role. The role was new and still not well understood internally or well resourced within the company. And while I was tasked with creating strategic partnerships with academic leadership, I had no marketing materials—nothing to leave behind to help steer the conversation, nothing to refer back to in order to inform any decision. *Ugh.* I figured I needed something to help steer the conversation, so I created a simple document that listed the products and their descriptions that I had to sell. I asked this leader to read my document and tell me if any of the products had strategic resonance.

As I watched him read, I had two contrasting experiences. Part of my awareness was focused on consciously praying that this leader would feel compelled to work with me on at least one of my products. I radiated Divine love to him, asking for the highest good to be present as I sat there waiting for his reaction. I also felt the pain from the milk engorging my breasts increasing with every passing minute. I had pads tucked securely in my bra to soak up any leaks, yet as the meeting continued, I could feel dampness; I knew I was leaking through my perfectly tailored silk blouse. I held my deep sadness inside for having to do something that certainly didn't align with my breasts, or, frankly, my heart.

As I subtly leaned down to hide my chest under the conference table, the grief within was hard to ignore. Thankfully, this academic leader wanted to partner around a math tutoring system I was selling, so at least I had that. The math software was truly transformational, and after my meeting with the Cal State executive, I made a conscious decision to try to change math remediation rates statewide. At the time, nearly sixty percent of incoming Cal State freshman could not place in for-credit, college algebra classes. Sadly, young people were graduating from high school knowing little more than basic arithmetic. I decided I was going to change that. And a few years later, I would be co-hosting math remediation summits across the state with this executive as my partner, sharing best practices around the use of my software and inspiring math educators to begin implementing this ground-breaking new approach to teaching mathematics.

If I had to work, I was going to find meaning in it.

My new job required near-constant travel. I was conscious of wanting to create as much new business as I could. Since the work was brand new, I figured I should prioritize strategic relationships close to home, so creating new partnerships in California became my focus. Lucky for me, California was the largest academic market in the country, so my territory was ripe with unrealized potential.

I found myself either driving or flying to universities' central offices every week and attending conferences to find as many avenues to get in front of academic leaders as I could. As I would cry myself to sleep in a hotel suite, I longed for my children and prayed that they were thriving in my absence.

Often alone, and often unhappy, my prayer and meditation practice was beginning to fade, and my old ways of coping were beginning to take hold—smoking and drinking. Not excessively, but I noticed I was using these as a way of coping with the stress. As time passed, it was becoming easier to be away from home than to be home. I felt an almost visceral distain for my husband, how he seemed to hold no impulse to financially care for our young children and me. I felt like he knew, unconsciously, that I would rise out of the ashes and make it work. My drive, born from trauma and the unbridled power of my parents, began to take hold once more. I was now a rainmaker at work, securing highly strategic partnerships mostly within the California State University system, still with little company support. I still had no marketing materials and trying to secure resources within my company to support my closed business was more challenging than closing the business itself. After hearing another "No!" from an internal executive about yet another deal, I was beginning to feel a bit like Sisyphus, destined to continue pushing a boulder up hill, only to have it roll down for eternity. Like Sisyphus, I kept pushing.

"Would you happen to have a box cutter?" I asked my neighbor at a conference, who, like me, was tasked with setting up and manning his own booth. He enthusiastically shared his tool, and as I looked up to see his company name in all caps on his booth banner, I said, "I have no idea what a Unicon is. What does your company do?" I was unloading boxes full of textbooks. I thought it was comical that my company still sent books to support the digital products and services I was selling, but I had learned to surrender to the disconnect and create my own brand. I could have gotten lost in thought about how misaligned my efforts were with my company's priorities and that all I wanted was to be with my kids, but instead I found myself charming a stranger as he described what his company was all about.

As I listened, an energy within me began to surge. My intuition always felt this way. As he spoke, I sensed that this company had the potential to be an incredibly valuable strategic partner. The rest of the conference was spent getting to know my neighbor, who already felt like a trusted friend. What I didn't know in that moment was that the connection I had just made was going to dramatically affect both my work life and my personal life. I was on the cusp of creating a powerful partnership that would end up in McGraw-Hill's annual report and the genius behind it would become my confidant. He would also become my lover. He would show me what it felt like to be well treated by a man, what nurturing gestures of care felt like, and ultimately what a man who loved a woman would be willing to do when met with dark confrontation.

Chapter 14. Rise and Fall

After the conference, I continued to stay in close touch with my new friend at Unicon. I learned at the conference that this small yet highly strategic company had helped an engineer at Cisco Systems build the largest global e-learning program: the Cisco Networking Academy. This educational program was implemented in over 150 countries, with close to a million active users. When Cisco was building the Internet, they lacked an educated labor force to support building and maintaining the emerging network. In response, a Cisco consulting engineer, George Ward, invented a solution to the problem by designing curricula that could teach the world how to support the networks that underlay the Internet and use the Internet itself to distribute the education and training. Brilliant. George was now holding the vision of using the same architecture that he had designed for teaching people about routers and networks to teach literally anything and everything else. George thought that if math, science, even English instruction, could be scaled similarly with an adaptive technology that he had patented, it could provide learners with customized instruction based on not only their learning style but also on what they were ready to learn, and he could impact educational outcomes globally. All he needed was content.

So George and I began holding private meetings with Unicon's introduction to plan a strategic partnership with McGraw-Hill that we both believed could change the world.

This partnership became my focus. Given its complexity and how little the current executives at McGraw-Hill seemed to know about academic technology, I began a quest to educate as many of them as I could about the power of this potential union. My commitment to this felt ministerial. I held a passion within me to make a difference, and I sensed this partnership could truly affect educational outcomes, just as the Network Academy had. I wasn't passionate about this because of what I could gain in terms of corporate advancement—that urge had left my consciousness long ago. If I had to be away from my two sons, all I wanted was to make a difference. And once it was understood by a gaggle of executives, I witnessed all the political maneuvering on the part of upper management to "own" a partnership that they hardly understood or had anything to do with creating—they just knew it was good. Two men were appointed to take the partnership to market, and I was given a "relationship management" role. The patriarchy was alive and well.

George and I had chemistry. He felt that I truly understood his vision and appreciated my consistent efforts to get my company strategically engaged. And I was attracted to his genius and his no-bullshit presence. He exuded strength, and I trusted him more with every interaction. As we began to sell our vision to state higher education systems together, the community college system of Hawaii became our first pilot customer. Every few months, we would fly to Honolulu to meet with higher education leaders, politicians, and other key stakeholders who supported our vision to create dynamic, student-centered curriculum with the same features as the Cisco Networking Academy, which had already proven that its architecture led to greater understanding of highly technical concepts. Given the abysmal math proficiency in the country, we focused our initial product development efforts on transforming the teaching of algebra. And Honolulu was an inspiring place to try to begin to change the world.

***

I hurried into the ABC convenience store, literally making a run for it, to briefly separate from the Cisco team and process what I was feeling. I grabbed my phone and called Marcy, my dearest friend, who also hired me into the business a decade before. "Oh, God, Marcy, what am I going to do? I feel as if Cupid literally just shot an arrow through my heart. I haven't felt this way since I first fell in love with Michael. Oh God. Help. The energy of this is potent and impossible to ignore." Marcy counseled me to just feel into the presence of what felt like a great love coming out of thin air.

Later that day, I sat at a long dining table surrounded by the product development team from Cisco, along with their integration partner, Edgepoint. I loved feeling the warm, gentle ocean breeze on my skin and the intoxicating fragrance of the plumeria flowers that grew like weeds everywhere. In that moment, I was happy. I was conscious that I was falling in love with George and, unlike other times in my past, I doubted I could hold this feeling back. My work felt profoundly purposeful. And while what I truly wanted was a happy marriage, a husband I could rely on, and an intact, harmonious family, I was beginning to own that the reality was far from my hope.

What I also now understand is that having to leave my children in order to work had created a split within me: my identity as I traveled far from home was not as a mother or even a wife. Those identities were too painful to embody while away from my children. So when I traveled for work, I became completely absorbed in making a difference and compartmentalized my pain.

George gazed intensely at me as we dined with the group. The energy between us was so alive. We tacitly knew what was happening. "Anyone want to go for a swim after dinner?" I asked the group as the song "Drift Away" played in the background. I had a festive cocktail in hand with one of those paper umbrellas and was feeling alive and a bit like I was on vacation. Each time we traveled to Honolulu, we stayed just across the street from Waikiki Beach.

"Yea, I'll swim. It is such a great night," George responded. *Only* George responded. My heart felt like it might literally split open.

I hurried back to my hotel room to freshen my makeup and put on my bathing suit. I got to the water a few minutes before George and, as he approached, I felt so alive, purposeful, radiant with a sense of mission, and a bit nervous. He walked towards me with strength and confidence. His body exuded masculinity and power. Six pack abs. A large chiseled chest. Broad, sculpted shoulders. As he waded into the water, he approached me, extending his arms and holding me as we felt the warm, almost holy, water lapping against our expectant skin. He gazed deeply at me and, with such sincerity, said, "Your commitment to my vision and the work you have put in to support it means so much. Thank you. And in return, please know I will always have your back." And he meant it. His words were like medicine. Medicine that I desperately needed. Medicine that helped me feel safe, held, and supported. As we waded further in the warm salt water, we kissed passionately. I was deeply in love.

I was also deeply conflicted. George and I began our long affair that night. And while I broke up with him almost monthly, because part of me felt it was so wrong, most of me needed him and the love he could so generously express to me. I stayed with him, through some of the most tumultuous circumstances I had ever created.

As George and I traveled together, evangelizing our corporate partnership, I felt deeply met. Met in the work, knowing that if both companies could execute the vision we held, we could truly change educational outcomes globally. I felt it. George was interested in all of me. He soaked up as much of me as he could. He was genuinely interested in understanding and trying to embody what I shared with him. My past, my spiritual education, my processes were of sincere interest to him. He began practicing what I shared with him. His interest in this part of me fueled a recommitment to my spirit, to my prayer, and to my meditative life. And as I recommitted, I was well served by my renewed appreciation for what sincerely held Divine love can do. Tapping into the force of creation was helping me create important partnerships and really moved the needle at work; I never worked more than twenty-five hours a week. The Divine energy I was connected to and my prayer were making things happen. It felt like magic. And I also recognized that my deception, my choice to lie to my husband, was creating an inner bifurcation. An inner split. And while it may sound odd, my relationship with George in some ways was improving my life at home. I could connect to more elevation within myself and that helped me feel somewhat more present at home with Michael and the boys. Yet, I wasn't being honest. My deception was in stark contrast to Divine expression. On the one hand I had remarkable access and on the other I was living a lie.

Michael and I were heading to Colorado for a family reunion. I was practiced at finding ways to be alone so I could call George. I hated this aspect of my life. It felt so deceptive and wrong. Mid-trip I decided to tell Michael how I felt about George. I told him I had fallen in love and didn't know what to do or how to reconcile it. Michael and I had had many conversations over the years about open marriage, about how the human heart is vast and certainly able to love more than one person. Sacred partnership is vital and ideal, yet I knew that wasn't really what I had with either man. I longed for a solution that could somehow not cause harm. But that simply wasn't available. I knew no matter what, given the choices I was making, I was going to hurt those I loved most.

Michael hardly responded to my sharing. I am sure he went numb. I had rejected him consistently over the years. His choices and how he often treated me triggered my childhood trauma. He was a mirror, though not a precise mirror, of my mother.

What I understand now is that Michael and I were a true gift to each other. The immense love that we had known once was real and true. And his dysregulation—his highs and lows—enabled me to feel just as I did as a child. And my rejection of him sexually, not feeling safe to share a bed with him at night, triggered his wounds around his mother, who had not been kind, loving, or affectionate with him. We were unconsciously creating a mirror so we could feel as we did as kids so we could heal it. I often wonder if we had been conscious of this, if we had applied our honest, deep conversations to this, if we had applied our spiritual wisdom and tools to this knowing, could we have made it? I will never know, but I think about it a lot, even now.

Since I had been honest with Michael about my feelings, a part of me now felt free to continue being with George. But that was the only piece I was honest about. I wasn't transparent about any aspect of this with Michael other than my feelings. I just sought an exit, needing to escape the pain of my home life seemingly the only way I could back then: by being dishonest and not facing the truth of my life at home.

Every trip with George felt electric. There was deep ease; for the first time, I felt taken care of by a man. George was generous, hard-working, visionary, and he loved me with abandon. In the morning in the hotel wherever we were that week getting ready to meet with academic leaders or politicians, George would head somewhere early to get me my favorite coffee. Not as a response to my asking, just an impulse within him to care for me. I know it sounds simple and common, but for me it was a first. He would often comment on how beautiful my eyes were as we gazed soulfully at each other. I remember thinking, *Same eyes, yet Michael has never commented on them*. I felt like George saw me, all of me, including my shadow, and he loved it all.

Our work partnership was getting complex. An executive at Cisco was promoted to be the General Manager of George's project and that mirrored the executives on my side promoted to run it. Neither knew what they were doing and both were motivated by power and ambition, not sincere care for or belief in the power of the Global Learning Network. The executive on George's side was disingenuous and slick. I knew this guy was unethical. I could feel it. And over time, George and I both watched him fire trusted team members who had worked for George for over a decade. George's boss wanted him out, and his influence was diminishing with his own people. Trusted engineers who had built the Academy program were being let go. Power on both sides was getting concentrated, and the people leading simply didn't know what they were doing. George and I were beginning to sense this was all going to go bust. And then George's boss reached out and told him he needed to meet. The message felt ominous.

"It is either GLN or Regan," Reza, George's boss said, confronting him with copies of phone logs that he had been given access to from his "friends" in IT. Reza knew we were in love. And as he threatened George, he was unknowingly underestimating him.

"Reza, when we first met, I think I mentioned I had *fuck you* money." Stock grants over the years had made George independently wealthy, having been with Cisco since almost the beginning. George now looked Reza right in the eye with an inner fury fueled by injustice, wrong action, and his deep love for me. "Fuck you, Reza. I quit!"

Visibly shaken, Reza responded, "What am I going to tell Chambers or Morgridge?"

"You should have thought about that before threatening me." Then George quietly, with a rage so pure it could melt ice, packed up his desk and left.

I then received a phone call from my boss, Jim, who kindly shared that Reza had called the president of McGraw-Hill telling him about the affair. After an internal meeting, the president asked Jim what they should do about it.

"Nothing, Ed. We are going to do nothing about it. It is none of our business, nor is it impacting our business."

I had now been working at McGraw-Hill for six years, but upon hearing this, I knew it was time to leave, though I had no idea what to do next. What I chose when confronted with hard things was to pray, so I pulled over on the side of the road, in my company Jeep, and gazed out the window at the gorgeous valley in the Santa Cruz Mountains, where redwood trees majestically reached for the heavens in a dense, lush rainforest-like scene. Somehow, I felt at peace. With the energy of George's grand gesture of love, how he chose to respond to Reza's threat, I felt deeply supported and safe somehow. George was driven to care for and protect me, and he had just proven it in such a dramatic way. In an instant, he was willing to leave a project that had defined his career. He was my knight in shining armor. My boss's response also felt like a great act of love.

Still on the side of the road, I closed my eyes and began to pray. I connected to my vast heart and activated a feeling and connection to gratitude and love, which was easy to access. I soaked in that energy for twenty minutes or so, and then I asked my higher self for a solution to my work dilemma. And I got one.

Call Gerry Hanley. Tell him you want to work for him. Tell him how you can help him with industry relations and oversee corporate vendor relationships to help him build innovative solutions for the state. The inner guidance felt deeply resonant and right. I checked to see if I had enough bars on my phone and then immediately called Gerry's cell and told him everything. "Gerry, I literally just came out of prayer and meditation knowing that I need to leave McGraw and asking what is in my highest good to do next. I was told to call you and tell you that I can help you and here's how." I then explained what I was directed to say.

"Regan, you are exactly right. I need you. Write your job description, and I will post it."

And so, for the next five years I worked for the California State University Chancellor's Office, helping to create innovative academic solutions with industry to support student success. And I convinced Gerry to hire George as his lead software architect.

While I had taken care to connect with Spirit to find a work solution that felt exciting and hopeful, I couldn't seem to apply the same process to finding a solution to my marriage. I unconsciously didn't want to hear what my higher intelligence would direct, so I simply never asked. I wasn't ready to leave him. I wasn't ready to break up my family. In the painful years that followed, I would finally reach the point where liberating myself from a marriage that didn't feel safe or supportive was the only way I could begin to find my way back to myself.

Chapter 15. Endings

When you deeply love someone who mirrors your childhood trauma, you hold onto hope like a lifeline. I wasn't conscious that the need I felt to stay with Michael was a way of not giving up on my mother. I know it sounds odd, but I truly believed if I loved him more or better or differently, he would show up differently. Just as I had with my mom.

As a child, I naturally accessed love as a way to feel safe. Almost as soon as I could write, I began a daily habit of doodling on my school folders the word "LOVE," in big, interconnected, bubble letters that reflected the hippie designs of the 1970s. I used the energy of love to bypass my pain, to bypass actually feeling the terror of my young life, and then I used my access to Divine love to bypass how much pain my marriage created. I kept thinking that if I just loved more, I could make it all better. When I did finally exit my marriage, it was not an act of love for Michael; it was an act of love for myself.

I don't blame Michael. He is not the villain in my story. Rather, what we shared was a vast love secured with the glue of a trauma bond. Anytime Michael showed me love or did something thoughtful, I would quickly breakup with George, hoping that Michael and I could find our way.

Years earlier, when my father was dying from cancer and my son, Ian, was an infant, I knew my father's death was coming soon. I was called to travel back to Missouri to see him and to say goodbye, to hold him as he lay in hospice, and to tell him how much I loved him and how much I had learned from him. I wanted us all as a family to travel together so I could say goodbye with Michael there to care for Ian. I needed support. But Michael refused to travel with us, not wanting to spend the money. So I traveled alone with Ian and arranged for a friend to drive a couple of hours to St. Joseph to help me with him. Ian was still breastfeeding exclusively, so I needed to have him near me. I felt uneasy knowing that Ian was with someone who was a stranger to him. As I lay in my Dad's hospice bed, I tried to soak in the love that was so present between us.

I felt torn, divided, and emotionally exhausted. I couldn't be fully present with my dying father because I sensed my baby was struggling in my absence. Having to leave my father's bedside, saying a final goodbye, to care for my baby felt like I was being split in two. I looked soulfully in my father's eyes and, as tears rolled down my cheeks, said, "I am so sorry Daddy, but I have to go now. Ian needs me." I told him again how much I loved him. We knew this was it.

The last thing my father said to me was, "Well, honey, it is always good to see you." And the meaning I heard was, *Don't put too much significance in this. I will always be with you. Have no doubt: we will see each other again.* Even in death, my father exuded a charisma like no other.

More than ten years later, as a gesture of his love, Michael traveled back to Missouri to collect personal effects of my father's, which were also things my selfish stepmother had no interest in and was willing to part with. Michael had apologized with such sincerity about not supporting me in saying goodbye to my dying father through a letter he wrote me, conveying his love and regret.

Upon receipt, I called George and told him I wanted to work on reconciling with my husband, who was "really trying to change."

This pattern would continue until a defining moment when I recognized the truth.

I was becoming someone I didn't recognize—someone who would lie with ease to hide the truth of my actions. As I became a shadow version of myself, I saw in real time how that was affecting my children. They both were adrift.

My older son, Connor, struggled significantly in high school. Drinking too much, stealing, and lying were common occurrences. Years later, he would write in his college application essays to the University of California how he had descended into his shadow during high school, losing his way due to his conflicted relationship with his father. And my younger son, Ian, so sensitive and empathetic, was not thriving at all. He was bullied consistently and his undiagnosed dyslexia inhibited his capacity to learn with ease in any school setting. He had few friends and was often overcome with feelings he couldn't regulate on his own. He and his father would have intense conflict, and I often found myself comforting my son from yet another near-violent conflict over nothing of true consequence. My life was descending into darkness, and I knew in my heart I could not continue as I was. It was too painful.

Michael and I separated, reconciled, and separated again. This reflected my innate desire not to break up my family. Any positive change would give me the false hope that it could work. If someone had told me years earlier that I would be grateful for my career, I wouldn't have believed them then—but boy was I grateful I was financially independent and able to support myself. It was ultimately my ticket out of a toxic union.

We were living apart yet trying to reconcile. Michael would come to my beach house after the children were in bed and we would make love and try to reconnect. I think we both sensed it felt forced, but we were trying.

Then, on a fateful day after a shared holiday meal, we began playing cards as a family. It was a simple game of poker, but Ian was ten and didn't really understand the game or know its rules. Michael ended up screaming at him for not understanding, which reminded me of how he had once screamed at him—calling him a "retard"—when he failed to learn to ride a bike. Just as I had during that moment with my mother when she was yelling at me at dinner and I bottom-lined her, I looked at Michael, folded my hands, and said, "I simply can't do this anymore. I am done."

It was a long time coming—and then, just like that, I was done. And to my surprise, I didn't reconcile with George either. I sensed that he was not my path forward either. I knew that I needed to learn how to stand on my own two feet, and I began the process of truly learning how. In forty-four years, I had never lived alone. I also knew I needed to find a way to both mourn and honor the twenty-five years Michael and I had lived together, twenty-two of them married, which represented over half my life.

My first step in alchemizing pain into self-acceptance was to write a eulogy to my marriage. I took pen to paper, with no intention to share it with Michael, just as a way to begin the process of transforming my grief, pain, sense of aloneness, and estrangement into meaning and acceptance.

> To our union, Michael,
>
> I love you. Our union provided the deepest love I have known. It also provided the deepest pain. You have been my greatest teacher. I was able to experience the full spectrum of human emotion. We experienced such joy, such profound union. We experienced such divide, such profound pain. You taught me so much as we grew up together. The love we shared helped me exit my violent, chaotic home and provided me the opportunity to create peace and harmony. But we

didn't know how. Neither of us had models worthy of modeling. We were lost, trying to somehow heal the trauma of our childhoods by providing a mirror to each other. A mirror that let us feel again how we felt as kids, but we didn't know it was that. After my awakening after another emotionally intense outburst of yours, I remember responding by coming to your office with a painting I bought that read, "Omnia Vincit Amor," which means *love conquers all* in Latin. I continued my pattern of offering unconditional love, thinking that it could change you and change us. I learned as the song says, "Sometimes love just isn't enough."

There is a part of me that wants to go back in time and rewrite our history. To bring the awareness of the now as opposed to who I was then. I know how much I hurt you. I wish I had had the inner sight early on to let you know why I behaved as I did. That I was desperately trying to exit my pain born from early childhood trauma. The impact of the eviction was deep. I could no longer trust you, my inner child perceived you as even dangerous, yet I loved you so intensely I could not imagine life without you, so I stayed in it. I was in it yet not fully, for I didn't feel safe.

I needed you to hold me safely. I needed you to create a safe place so I could heal. I needed your protection. I needed you to take care of me. You simply didn't know how. I don't blame you. I know you tried. Just like me at the time, your wounding predominated you. You didn't think it was your role to care for me really. You knew I could take care of myself. But that wasn't what I needed. I needed you to create safety yet what you knew how to create was turbulence and conflict. And I responded sometimes with dysregulation too. But more often I responded as I had learned to in order to survive. Access love. Radiate love. Use the energy of love to leapfrog over the pain. I truly believed we could somehow make it.

I am so profoundly sorry for exiting the marriage with George as I did. But that wasn't why our marriage failed. Our marriage failed because of what remained traumatized within us. It will remain my prayer and my greatest hope that you find a way to heal. To build an intimate, safe harbor for our sons who are now adults but still need a stable, present, and safe father.

I marveled at how you were able to build your investment advisory practice again. Becoming President of the Board of a bank. Becoming treasurer of our community foundation. You could exude such power, such intellect. I was so proud of you. Yet your inner restlessness, just like my father's, encouraged you to be reckless and invest in speculative real estate. *You failed big.* The bankruptcy, your inability to care for your children, either emotionally or financially, was heartbreaking. They both needed you and you simply weren't present. Even as Ian descended into addiction, your focus remained on yourself. I remember when it was your weekend to care for him, I would drive by your home late at night and you weren't there. Ian needed your protection; you to hold strong boundaries for him, but you chose to focus on yourself, your pain, and your relationship with Erin. You watched me as I homeschooled Ian while holding a full-time job. It wasn't you who went to school to protect him from bullying during recess. It was me. I was holding so much, and you simply didn't see it or offer much in assistance. I often wonder what you see, what you own, what you remember. I own that my unhealed self ran my show. I found an exit in George; he modeled for me what being cared for looked like, felt like. I will always be grateful for him, for he was the catalyst I needed to finally leave you and venture out on my own.

Such sweet moments each evening as you and I created ritual for the children, practicing gratitude, using sage in sweet ceremony. Remembering how you held me during childbirth with such love and commitment. That was the man I needed everyday. Your acceptance of me after my awakening was generous. Your willingness to move to support my heart directive to work at HeartMath was inspiring and hopeful. But in the end, I needed consistent safety in order to finally heal so I needed to leave you to create that first myself.

Your love of nature was inspiring. I loved our hikes, our time in the Rockies, and I appreciate so much how you infused your love of nature with conscious activities for our boys. That love has informed them and they now want time in nature as a way to reflect, connect, and restore.

I want to believe in your goodness. Yet the choices you continue to make challenge me in doing so. Please find your way. Our sons need you. And I need you. Your trauma isn't your fault. Your healing, though, is your responsibility. I will know you have healed when you are able to build a close, safe and emotionally intimate relationship with our sons. And I am cheering you on, praying for you everyday. Each time I teach yoga now while closing with a Metta prayer it is you that I bring to my mind's eye. "May you be happy. May you be healthy. May you have peace. May you have ease."

Thank you for loving me as you did. It was exactly what I needed in order to finally have enough pain that I had no other option than to learn how to heal and transform it.

And with the words of this eulogy written, I laid my marriage to rest.

Chapter 16. On My Own

The first year on my own, 2011, I made $279,000. I share that not from pride, but rather to acknowledge what it took to live comfortably and support my sons. My income reflected where I was putting my energy. Given that Michael was on the verge of bankruptcy, sending me monthly spreadsheets dividing our shared costs down to the penny, it was clear that I needed to rely solely on myself. And in contrast to how I approached my work, in the past I was internally more casual that I had ever been before. My spiritual practices held in deep focus, and I was able to attract prosperity with relative ease. I held in my awareness the intention to take everything I had learned and apply it to creating a new life on my own terms and in my own way, unencumbered by childhood trauma. I was feeling hopeful and enlivened by this fresh start.

I no longer worked for the California State University system, having returned to the private sector in a business development leadership role for an early-stage education technology company. Spirit had led me to a beautiful rental that had been a vacation rental for years prior and the sweet landlord offered to let me use anything there for my daily needs. So I didn't need to spend money on creating a new household, with a few exceptions. My landlord also lived on site in another house in the back and his presence was a comfort. One night a ravaging storm came through and we lost power. Within minutes, he was knocking on my door with battery powered lights, asking, "Anything I can do?" I felt deeply at ease and protected. Spirit had my back.

My focus was on my work, my boys, and my spiritual practices. I was determined to continue to excavate the traumas held within my tissues and became more and more disciplined. I prayed consistently throughout each day, asking for my highest good to be illuminated. My prayer was simple, "Dear God, beloved angels, guides, and ancestors, I ask to be an instrument of the highest good. I ask for the resources, people, and insights I need to fulfill my mission to be present. I am grateful for your help, and so it is!"

I wasn't interested in dating. Succeeding in work and creating a safe haven for my sons was more than enough. Frankly, I had no interest in men. I put my energy into my spiritual life and my continued healing, my work, and my sons, and time with other resonant women brought me great joy. My closest friend, Icasiana, helped me decorate my new home—thankfully she lived just a few blocks away. We would often text and have impromptu get togethers, like time with my mother, we would smoke organic cigarettes, talk deeply, and laugh with abandon. I felt peace and hope.

The only drag on my system was working for an abusive CEO, who threatened physical violence in meetings and easily lost his temper. In some ways, his frequent dysregulation coupled with his powerful intellect and substantial charisma reminded me of my past and let me know that if he was in my life triggering me as he did, there was work to do—or at least strong boundaries to create.

"You know, Regan, if this was my deal, it would be done by now," my CEO fumed on our call about a substantial partnership I was working on. Perhaps it was my disciplined practice fueling my courage, or perhaps I simply had had enough of his bullshit, but I held no fear as I quickly responded.

"No, Sean. The reason this is taking so long is the CEO thinks you are a complete asshole and has strong reservations about working with you." I knew in that moment I needed to find another job. And while I appreciated that I worked from home, which enabled me to be more present for the boys, I began my job search. What I didn't realize was that the choice I would soon make would be essential to my future, to my mission, and to finding a profound love unlike any I had ever known.

But first I needed to be alone and play.

Chapter 17. A Bridge

On the eve of my forty-fourth birthday, I felt free. The boys were with their dad that weekend, and I felt an inner liberation as I touched up my makeup, getting ready to take myself to my favorite wine bar to celebrate. My peaceful excitement had become my steady, inner state. Living on my own for the first time felt profoundly purposeful. I was heading to Soif solo for some elegant wine and food—not meeting friends, rather, celebrating my aloneness.

    I called the sommelier, who had become a close girlfriend, to let her know I was on my way and asked her to reserve a spot at the bar for me. As I continued getting ready, I reflected on my lack of interest in dating. I had been in a relationship with a man, almost without interruption, since I was seventeen. I had earned, and needed, a break. I decided to dress up a bit, wearing an elegant, long, black blouse with an asymmetrical edge, black skinny jeans, and dramatic large silver hoops adorned my ears. I took more time than usual to curl my hair in beachy waves. As I gazed in the mirror, I was pleased and felt conscious love for myself as I reflected on how much had changed and how much I was changing. I prayed that I would have a fantastic night and asked Spirit, as I did daily now, to bring me insights, resources, and people to support my highest good.

As I opened the door, the winter air had a definite chill, though winters in Santa Cruz weren't really winters. I put on an elegant coat of light black wool and ventured out.

As I entered the wine bar, I sensed people staring at me. Most of the time I just tuned it out, but tonight, I noticed. I wondered to myself as I headed to the bar, *Do we emit some kind of different pheromone when we are single*? Well, whatever it was, I didn't care. I was committed to being alone and wasn't there to meet a man; I was there to celebrate myself at my favorite place. Jen, the sommelier had placed a tent card—RESERVED—at a spot at the bar for me. I sat down and a beautiful, radiant, blonde woman sitting next to me exclaimed, "We were wondering who the VIP was. Had no idea Soif reserved bar stools!" This woman felt different than most in this small, bohemian town. She had a sophistication about her. She struck up a conversation with me, as her husband sat back, listening to us get acquainted. I think she sensed I grew up somewhere else and began to ask me typical questions regarding my work and history. We had an electric connection. Then she enthusiastically proclaimed, "You need to meet my best friend. He is wonderful. Good looking, smart, and very funny!"

I responded with an emphatic, "No thanks. I haven't been single for long and I really have no interest in dating right now."

She was undeterred. She kept repeating her mantra, "You must meet my best friend." Then, against my explicit permission, she took a photo of me and texted it to him. I was a bit bugged, but she was so charming, we continued chatting. She learned I grew up in St. Louis and she then shared that when she was married to her first husband, she lived there and worked in restaurants.

"Where did you work?" I asked, feeling that some synchronicity might be at play.

"I tended bar for awhile and waited tables at Annie Gunns."

"I loved that place! You wouldn't happen to know Scott Bostick by chance? He used to be the bar manager there for years."

She got a mischievous smile and answered, "Yes, I know Scottie—he trained me." I then explained that Scott was my best friend in high school. At this, she almost jumped out of her seat and smartly blurted out, "Well since I know your best friend, won't you at least meet mine?" I couldn't ignore the synchronicity, the statistical improbability of the moment. I surrendered.

"Okay. Sure. I will meet him." She texted him to come to Soif and, ten minutes later, an adorable, tall man with eyes that twinkled was standing behind me asking me funny questions. I felt something—a fun aliveness in our connection. The wine was warming me, and I decided to drop my guard. It felt like Spirit had intervened and, given my prayer before I left the house, I decided to see where this new connection would take me.

Sven and I dated for five months. Not seriously and not often. I was busy with work and had the boys every other weekend, so spare time was sparse. I didn't want to introduce him to my children, knowing from the beginning that it wasn't more than a resonant fling. He was literally the funniest man I had ever known, and laughing with him was potent medicine. He had a job managing buildings for the local university and wrote a smart comedic column for our local paper. On our first date we met on the cliffs overlooking Monterey Bay. He held me so tenderly. We had powerful sexual chemistry. He asked me insightful questions about my past. After hearing about Mike and George he quipped, "Well, Regan, I guess no one could say you have a type." I was definitely the first corporate executive he had dated and when he learned about my awakening and early spiritual education, he admitted he couldn't relate. I certainly wasn't his type either, but for five months, it worked. He helped me embrace being single and gave me the experience of dating, which I hadn't done in decades. I broke it off just after Mother's Day because I knew in my heart it wasn't going anywhere substantial, and I felt I was wasting time and energy with him. One of the last things he said to me was, "It makes sense. I love the show *Dexter* and you are pure sunshine and light." We kissed one last time, and I silently acknowledged my gratitude to the Divine for bringing us together. He was a fun, lighthearted bridge from my dysfunctional past to the coherent, loving future I held inside as a prayerful possibility.

That said, what was coming was definitely something my psychic self had no sense of. In fact, if someone had told me what was coming, I wouldn't have believed them.

Chapter 18. A True New Beginning

Even though I was making great money, I decided—given my toxic CEO—to apply to a competitor, managing relationships and securing distribution agreements with college textbook publishers. An exciting, well-capitalized start up funded by Marc Andreessen, the inventor of the first widely used internet browser, was creating a next-generation digital textbook platform with embedded video and assessment, as opposed to the boring, static PDFs that dominated the market. I was excited to apply.

A week later, I was offered the job. Given that I was still committed to my daily prayer and meditation, asking for the resources, people, and insights to support my highest good, I sensed that the ease of getting this new, well-paying job was informed by Divine purpose. I was right.

About eight months had passed since I had broken off my casual relationship with Sven when I decided to put more intention into finding a partner. While I enjoyed certain aspects of being single—namely, doing whatever I wanted in my spare time when I didn't have the children—there was a part of me that longed for meaningful connection and support. Being a single mom with significant work responsibilities was draining. My former *I want to do it all by myself* attitude was fading as I continued to heal and connect more inner dots. It was becoming clearer that my independence was a trauma response. I was also beginning to realize that something as fundamental as my personality was also more a response to trauma than something actually innate. My former ways of being were beginning to feel awkward and unnatural. I was changing. My best friend was my relationship to the unseen world, to my inner guidance, and to the Divine itself. While I wasn't lonely, per se, because I held that awareness so deep within me, I was beginning to acknowledge that it was time to find a true, healthy mate.

When I was a young girl at Forsyth, we were taught how to manifest our heart's desire. The process was simple: visualize what you want and feel into as many dimensions of it as you can—what it looks like, sounds like, and feels like. Bring that image vibrantly into your mind and radiate a sincere feeling of gratitude for it. Not gratitude because you didn't have it and now do (that has a vibrational frequency of lack), rather inherent gratitude for it—the joy it brings, the resonance it offers. Once firmly in mind, encapsulate it—put it in an imagined balloon or place it on an imagined log on a riverbank—and then watch it float away in your mind's eye. As you release it completely to the Divine, feel a knowing in your heart that unseen forces will help you make this a reality. In fact, it already is a reality because you visualized it, felt gratitude for it, and released it. Then exclaim, "And so it is!" I remembered this childhood lesson and had used it routinely in business. Now I decided to use it to manifest a wonderful man.

I wrote on a piece of paper a list of attributes that were important to me in my partner, which stood in sharp contrast to what I had known. I wrote: "My man is: stable, kind, generous, smart, honest, loving, unselfish, able to commit, a dedicated father, a success in business." For some reason I didn't include anything about his spiritual life. I guess I assumed if he possessed all those qualities, he was evolved in his spiritual journey. And interestingly I did not name anything about his physicality. I guess in my heart I knew that the external truly didn't matter much. I then placed the paper under my mattress and slept on it, radiating love and gratitude to this man, whoever he was, each night before I fell asleep.

At work in the new job, I was tasked with securing distribution agreements with all college textbook publishers, while also attaining content so my company could pursue research and development for the innovation they were creating. Given that non-majors biology was a big course with ample opportunity for embedded videos and other dynamic features to enliven the reading experience, my job was to get a major publisher to offer their content on a piloted basis so my company could innovate and experiment. I decided to approach McGraw-Hill, given that my former boss, Jim, had been promoted to president a year after I had resigned. I was confident he would help me. That was his nature. I remembered fondly the time he offered to babysit my sons at a company conference so that my husband and I could have a night out. Certainly not a common practice for bosses, but that was just who Jim was—generous and kind.

Jim and I had many phone conversations focused on my work priorities, and while it had been seven years since I had worked for him, he was happy to help. As I waited on hold for him to come on the line, I smiled to myself, remembering a funny, yet odd, quick conversation my mother and I had when I first started working for him in 2001. After my first manager's meeting in Chicago, I flew back home to St. Louis to see my mom and took her to a Cardinals' game. I still don't understand why my mother was passionate about baseball. The *Baseball Encyclopedia* sat next to her bed, and she read it from cover to cover. At the time, I was especially miserable in my marriage, and as we drove to the stadium she blurted out, "What about Jim Kelly?"

Given that she had never met him or spoken to him, I was confused. *What was she asking?* So I answered, "Mom, I don't understand the question."

She then repeated, "What about Jim Kelly?"

I gave her a contemptuous stare, picking up on what she was implying. "Mom, repeating the question doesn't make it any clearer."

She then retorted, "He is obviously crazy about you. He keeps hiring you, doesn't he?"

I emphatically countered, "No, Mom, Jim hired me because I am very good at what I do!"

She then playfully exclaimed, "I don't think that's it!"

Jim finally got on the line and we visited for a few minutes, talking about work politics. I casually mentioned that I was flying to New York City the following week for a series of meetings. He then quickly let me know that he was also going to be in New York for a board meeting. "We should have dinner, since we will both be there." Made sense to me. I told him to come to the W in the theater district around 7:00 and we would walk somewhere and grab a bite. I thought nothing of it. He was my former boss, helping me in my new role at a start-up, and we happened to be in New York at the same time.

As I sat at the bar at my hotel, I anxiously awaited his arrival because I was hungry. I called him, impatiently asking where he was since he was late. His driver was just heading through the tunnel and would be there soon. A financier was hitting on me, letting me know he was rich and blah, blah, blah. I couldn't wait for Jim to arrive so I could get the heck out of there and away from this obnoxious man. Just in time, I saw Jim staring at me from across the room, his heavy navy coat sheltering him from the cold outside. I quickly paid my check and walked towards him, feeling nothing other than relief. I was hungry and wanted to get away from the bar scene. We hugged and ventured out in the cold toward a small Italian restaurant nearby. I was not attracted to him, though over time at McGraw he had demonstrated his creative brilliance and his unwavering support for me, so I deeply appreciated him.

We had met the first time when I was twenty-three at Prentice Hall. We had been to countless meetings together and even though there were always evening parties and receptions at national and regional meetings, I had never seen Jim with an alcoholic drink in his hand. So, I was shocked over dinner as he ordered a rum and Coke about every fifteen minutes. Well, maybe I'm exaggerating, but he was drinking . . . a lot. We spoke about business. He had confided in me just before the trip that he had been demoted due to a reorganization. Upper management had gotten rid of all the divisional presidents and even though he was the only one they chose to retain, he was now in a senior business development role. I had received an email from him a few days before I left for New York and the subject line read: "Help me find my next life." He wanted my help finding a new job. He was clearly unhappy at work, and I sensed unhappy in most dimensions of life. I was encouraging him as we dined, letting him know how lucky any company would be to have his creative, strategic brilliance. He had increased revenue at McGraw by almost a half a billion dollars when he was president, and he had initiated and developed many innovations in the industry over the years. We exhausted the business topics of conversation, so I playfully asked him to read my Plenty of Fish dating profile. I had decided to use a free dating service, figuring the Divine could use a tool like that to help me find a partner. "You've known me a long time Jim, do you think this captures me authentically?" He ordered another drink.

Jim is an introvert with a playful side and a great sense of humor. I always felt like he was secretive and guarded, but as he continued to drink, he became more animated and, I sensed, more like himself. Jim is very tall, 6' 4" I guessed, and didn't take great care of his body. He was overweight and had clearly neglected himself. I thought of my father and remembered joking with him as a teen, telling him he treated his body as if its only function was to carry around his head. Jim seemed similar. As dinner ended and he paid the check, Jim asked if I wanted to head to Hurley's bar for a night cap and I said, "Sure!" I was having fun getting to know him on a more personal level. He was fun to talk to. He reminded me that when I had resigned from McGraw, I was drinking a cosmo, smoking a cigarette, and had boldly told him that if he lost fifty pounds women would fight over him. I had no memory of saying that, though it sounded like me. He let me know that he had taken my advice and had lost that weight. Given that he still appeared overweight, I quickly responded, "I should have said eighty pounds, but that just sounds mean!"

We sat at the bar at Hurley's and Jim ordered another rum and Coke. He was clearly drunk, but a playful, fun drunk. There was a lull in the conversation. Frankly, I do not remember what we were just talking about, but my memory is that it was feeling deep, intimate, and personal. Then, out of the quiet, fueled by rum and Coke, he began to tell me how he had always felt about me. That I was the most fascinating person he had ever known—so smart, beautiful, and confident—and that he had always harbored a deep love for me.

I was shocked. Talk about someone expert at compartmentalization. I never picked up on any vibe. And I certainly had never felt that way about him. I then remembered that moment with Mom. *Yet again, her intuition was spot on*! He then leaned in and sweetly asked, "Would it be okay if I kissed you?"

And without thinking I said a lighthearted, "Sure!"

His kiss was the most tender, the most generous, the most loving kiss I had ever known. It didn't feel passionate, or at least not passion as I thought I had known in my past, rather it felt like peace. It felt like safety. I wondered to myself if this was what love truly felt like. As I reflected on this moment in the days that followed, I was reminded of one of my favorite verses from the Bible, in Corinthians 13:4-7: "Love is patient and kind. Love is not jealous or boastful or proud or rude. It does not demand its own way.

It is not irritable, and it keeps no record of being wronged. It does not rejoice about injustice but rejoices whenever the truth wins out. Love never gives up, never loses faith, is always hopeful, and endures through every circumstance."

That evening, my journey to truly understanding what love was began. And for many years, I would fight it, not trusting it, as I waited anxiously for a shoe to drop or for him to finally reveal who he truly was, as opposed to the deeply committed, kind, generous, stable, unselfish man that I was experiencing. My wounded inner child mistrusted him for a long time, but at least I was somewhat conscious of that and, with the safety and quality of love he provided, I was able to heal and be catalyzed, in time, to live a life I had only imagined was possible. And most of all, he would equip me to live a life of service as I had been called to live some thirty years earlier, when I had dramatically awakened. All of it, I would learn, was exactly what I needed. No regrets, no one to blame, rather a life that ultimately brought us together in such a profound union that I wouldn't want to change any of what had preceded it. It would all fit together like a giant, complex puzzle. He was my missing piece.

Chapter 19. Transitions

Jim began visiting as often as he could when the boys were with their dad. Michael and I alternated weekends, and I was clear in myself and to Jim that until I knew for certain what this was and whether I wanted to commit to it long-term, there would be no integration of him with the boys. The boys were still reeling from the separation, and Connor was showing signs of deep internal disturbance. He struggled with sleep and with the truth. He was stealing. I was overcome with worry and guilt, feeling responsibility for his struggle and my contribution to it. It wouldn't be until ten years later that I would learn of the unspeakable trauma he had endured as a child, which—in hindsight—explained it all. But for now, the newness of being on my own and the hope and promise it represented was fading; what I was seeing and feeling now was more chaos and pain.

As I sat at my desk, a cool urban vibe permeated the office. I had recently accepted a position as Vice President of Sales for a pre-revenue, early-stage, education technology company in San Francisco led by a charismatic Black woman whose sense of mission about helping college students showcase their achievements with beautiful portfolio technology inspired me. My phone vibrated and, as I glanced at it, I saw a number I didn't recognize. I sensed trouble. I exited into the hallway and answered, "Hello, this is Regan."

"Yes, ma'am, this is Safeway calling. We have your son here in our possession. We caught him stealing a bottle of liquor, which he hid under his jacket. We are choosing not to press formal charges but do need you to come and get him since he is a minor."

Given that I was at least two hours away from Santa Cruz, I quickly responded. "You will need to call his father. I work in San Francisco." As I gave her his number, a fury climbed within me. I found myself not angry with my son, but rather angry with his father. Of course Connor wouldn't have him as a first responder to this. There was no trust and little emotional connection between them. Connor repeatedly shared with me how he didn't feel safe with his dad and how estranged he felt. I raged within, wondering how the hell I was going to teach my son to be an honest, healthy man in the absence of a father who was either of those things. I wanted to cry as I hung up the phone. I hardly knew my colleagues, so I told them my son was sick and I needed to return home. I would finish my day's work there. As I walked to my car, I wept. On the one hand, life felt hopeful given what had begun with Jim. Yet the lack of health in both of my boys felt all-consuming. *How am I going to work at the level required, spending at least five hours a day commuting, while helping my sons heal and process the break up of our family*? I had no answers. I had only my prayer.

Ian was struggling too—in school, bullied routinely, not protected by his teachers who were convinced he was incapable of learning and had expelled him from the fifth grade. I had recently been elected to the board of the school and my purpose was to bring accountability to teacher performance. I knew in my heart that expelling Ian was more of a response to me than to him. I was overwhelmed with worry, grief, and a sense of responsibility that part of his inner struggle, like Connor's, was due in part to the choices I had made. And while I had compassion for myself, I was determined to create a safe haven for them, filled with love, latitude, and unconditional acceptance. I just didn't yet know how.

I was grateful that Connor and I had a deep, seemingly unbreakable, bond. He was conceived just days after I had awakened. I trusted that in time he would find his way. That was my prayer then and continues to be. I knew in my heart that his profound wisdom, which he demonstrated readily when he was little, was who he was, and the rest was trauma not yet processed or acknowledged. He and I would have deep talks late into the night as we sat on my big, comfy bed. He was fairly open with me about his inner demons, and I loved him as unconditionally as I could. I sought treatment for him with a holistic physician who prescribed a series of supplements to help him find balance emotionally and to find a way to restful sleep. I am grateful to this day for the wisdom that this doctor embodied, for it transformed my son from someone who thought he was mentally ill to someone who could find some inner resolution.

Ian felt in some ways like a stranger to me. His entire life I had been focused on work—at first because I needed to provide for us when he was an infant, and then over time because I knew it was the only way out of my turbulent marriage. I loved Ian deeply, yet acknowledged that due to circumstances, we did not have the same kind of bond that Connor and I shared. And while Ian benefited from the love and consistent support of Max, our fantastic nanny who had worked for us since Ian was three, I knew in my heart that part of Ian's struggle was due to my absence. I was determined to find a way to change that. *How do I have a life where I can be more present for him, for both boys, while still taking care of the economics?*

Michael had moved south of Santa Cruz to Aptos to be closer to Ian's new school, Chartwell. I deeply appreciated Michael's willingness to do so, since I needed to accommodate my lengthy San Francisco commute. After Ian was expelled from his school, and with a diagnosis of his severe dyslexia in hand, we enrolled him in a school in Monterey, an hour or so from Santa Cruz, which specialized in working with students with learning differences. Life was increasingly complex, and I was extremely stressed trying to find a way to make it all work. And it wasn't working. I was relieved that Ian was thriving at his new school, learning innovative strategies to overcome his dyslexia, loving the new neighborhood where he and his Dad lived, and making some much needed friends with neighborhood boys.

But Michael's looming bankruptcy was straining him. Whatever he had done was apparently worthy of litigation, and some investors he had recruited for speculative real-estate deals were threatening to sue him. They were closing in. A year or so after Michael had moved to the new home in Aptos, where Ian was thriving, I reluctantly answered the phone when I saw Michael's name on the caller ID. After a few minutes of catching up, Michael then confided, "Re, I need to move and find a cheaper place to live."

My stomach churned with stress as I began to process what this would mean for Ian—and for me. Ian loved his new friends and the safety and beauty of the neighborhood. I knew what Michael's announcement represented for Ian. Another change, another event that would traumatize him. Upon hearing the news, I knew in my heart that I would figure out how to take over his lease and move south to Aptos, even though it would mean adding about two hours to my commute. Given how my choices had impacted Ian, I committed to not contributing any more to his suffering. My lease was ending the following month. I hired someone to help me move, said a grateful goodbye to my generous landlord, and settled into Michael's rental home. I appreciated the beauty of my surroundings. The ocean roared just across the street. Seascape, as my new neighborhood was called, had a calm, coherent energy about it; it was much more peaceful than Santa Cruz, with restaurants and an organic market a short walk from the house. I was determined to build a life there. To stay there. No more moving. I was committed to supporting my sons as best I could, while figuring out whether or not I wanted to create a life with Jim as my partner. I continued to pray for my highest good and for the highest good for my beloved sons.

Spending five hours in the car each day, figuring out how to make meals, helping with homework, while being responsible for revenue generation for a Silicon Valley start-up was taking a significant toll. And while I remained disciplined in my spiritual practice, I was beginning to doubt whether I could sustain it all. I sometimes doubted that my spiritual practice could do anything to help my sons.

The only stable constant was Jim's presence and abiding love. Yet I still mistrusted it, often finding reasons to doubt. I resisted surrendering to his love. I was conscious that my trauma was still active in my system and that trusting him, or any man for that matter, was still foreign to me. All I felt I could do was pray for resolution. I asked God everyday to show me the highest path forward. I asked God to remove obstacles within me so I could make a decision about Jim that was reflective of my heart's wisdom and nothing else.

One night, I wept in Jim's arms as I revealed to him how overwhelmed I felt. How I didn't know how I could continue, as I was, how the stress was unbearable, how I felt like my children deserved so much better. I wanted somehow to be more present for them. It was so clear how much they both needed more of me. And while I was still resisting Jim's love to a degree, his consistency, his stability, and his generosity was medicine. My resistance to it took the form of judgment. My wounded self was looking for reasons not to trust him and it was relentless in its point of view that we were not aligned. He was conventional in so many ways and my brokenness used it as evidence that he wasn't the right man for me. As he held me that fateful night, holding me as I wept and let go, his gaze felt unconditional. I sensed how different he was than any man

I had ever been intimate with. When I consciously let my guard down, like I was in that moment, taking deep breaths, I would say to myself, "I am safe." Affirming my safety allowed me to let him in, to allow myself to be loved and cared for.

And then he asked me a question. A question I had never been asked. "Why don't you let me take care of you?"

I recoiled in response. My initial internal reaction was a resonant, "Hell no!" I abruptly exited his arms, almost offended by his question. Then realizing where my response originated from, I took a deep breath and replied, "Thank you, love, that is something I will really need to think about."

"Take all the time you need," he responded. "I am not going anywhere."

Chapter 20. Surrender

I continued to reflect deeply on Jim's question, listing the pros and cons as if a list would lead to resolution. I wanted to ensure, somehow, that Jim understood me, my past, and how I was raised and educated. I wanted to be transparent about the paranormal experiences that had dominated my life. How I had learned to exit my body at will and how knowing how to do that let me know, without reservation, that we are all eternal energy housed in a shell called the body. Part of me thought if I shared it all, he would run. And that part of me wanted him to. Yet mostly I just wanted him to know me, to accelerate his understanding of me. Given that commitment to each other underlay his question, I thought it was only right that he know more of who I was, what I valued, and what I hoped we could create in sacred relationship.

So I wrote a short autobiography. Its pages detailed my education at Forsyth, the entities that I would see as a child, my ability to hear and see things that most do not, my dramatic awakening, my beliefs, my other paranormal experiences, and how a traumatic childhood coupled with the experience of my first marriage had me mistrusting. How my inability to trust readily showed up in unexpected ways, interfering with my ability to love and be loved. As I read what I had written, I felt that it was a vulnerable, authentic sharing of who I was and what I had known.

One sunny afternoon I handed it to Jim and asked him to read it. He smiled, read the few pages, looked at me tenderly and said very little. What I do remember him saying was that he knew most of it already. I had apparently told him most of it over the year we were seeing each other, yet I had remembered little of those conversations. I had come to accept that, like my mother, my memory was different from most people's. I am not sure exactly why that is, but I think unconscious channeling has something to do with it. Jim reassured me that all of my past experiences made me who I was and that who I was to him was the greatest love he had known. He response was so deeply comforting. Months later, I told him yes. I was ready. His offer was unlike any I had ever received.

My inner guidance had said an enthusiastic *YES*, but the rest of me still felt uncertain. In time I would learn that allowing him to love and care for me would bring profound blessings. My *yes* would grow with more time and healing. Jim provided an opportunity to heal more completely, to be of service, to build a strong, intimate relationship with Ian, while bringing much needed stability, unconditional love, and generosity to us all. He also gave me the precious opportunity to love him. A man so worthy of love, made of such goodness, that loving him became another element of my spiritual practice. I was learning how to heal and how to love. And as if the universe wanted to make sure I knew I was making the right decision, when my divorce papers finally arrived after the obligatory six month waiting period that California requires, I opened the envelope to see the date—June 12—the date the papers were filed, stamped all over the front page of the filing. Jim's birthday.

A year or so after taking over Michael's lease, Jim began to incrementally move in. I kidded him that I was giving him a drawer. Each visit, he would leave a bit more behind. The boys seemed to like him, though I sensed they both thought he was quiet and reserved—in definite contrast to their father—so they seemed unsure how to connect.

Also, they were busy. Ian continued to improve at his school; despite his dyslexia, he was being rebuilt as a learner from the inside out. Finally understood by his teachers, his self-confidence improved. His teachers reinforced that he was capable and smart; he simply needed tools to help him decode words. My sense was that the school was giving him, more than anything else, love and acceptance. I was hopeful that the combination of the school, a stable home, and friends in the neighborhood would continue to help Ian feel better about himself. Connor was taking classes at the local community college, with the intent to transfer in time to a university, and worked most days so I didn't see him much. Life had more ease. I could bring my focus to homemaking and parenting. I could finally exhale.

Renting homes in Santa Cruz County was inherently unstable. Leases, time and again, that I thought would be long term would change in an instant. One day I learned from the owner of my rental home that when the lease was up in a few months, he would be putting the house on the market. I didn't blame him. The housing market was hot, and I would have made the same choice. But this change in circumstances begged the question, *Now what*?

Jim wanted to buy us a home. He saw it as a good investment given how real estate seemed to be always appreciating near the coast, and he wanted us all to have a home that wouldn't change. *Our* home. The boys had moved four times as children, after Michael and I had sold our first California home, and we had been renting ever since. The hope and stability of a family home that was ours held deep resonance. I was still internally reluctant; my capacity to trust was a significant constraint, yet I was conscious of it. I figured since all healing begins with self-awareness, at least I had that. I shared with Jim that ideally we would find a home within a few blocks of the rented house. I wanted consistency for Ian.

And then Michael called. "Re, I am going to move back to St. Louis. I need support of family, and I want to create a new start there." Or something like that.

My heart sank. A mix of emotions stirred, but what was most present was anger. *Could the man think of anyone other than himself? How was Ian, or Connor for that matter, going to learn to be men with a father who lived thousands of miles away?* He clearly assumed I would just adapt. And he was right. I decided almost in that moment that I would be moving too. I simply couldn't tolerate the idea of Ian having an absent father at the age of thirteen.

I shared the news with Jim and, within a week, we flew to St. Louis to find our new home. Thankfully I had dear friends who still lived there and the schools were good, with many alternatives to public education, so I was confident I would find both my way and a way for Ian to continue to get the support he needed for his dyslexia. Since Connor was now in college with aspirations to move to L.A., I trusted that he would continue to create his adult life, even if I was further away.

Jim and I searched Zillow, narrowed down the parts of town best suited for Ian's education, and made our plans. I enjoyed sharing my hometown with Jim, who had no hesitancy about moving there. He said he didn't care where he lived, as long as he lived with me. As we were returning from our house-hunting trip, Michael called as we were waiting at the gate at the airport. He had received a rather tepid response from his family about moving back and saw it as a sign that he shouldn't move. *Ugh.*

"Okay. Michael. This needs to be it. I want to root myself with certainty and, should you decide to change your mind, I will not be adapting again. I will be remaining in Aptos." I closed my eyes after saying a curt goodbye to him on the phone and prayed. Prayed for a home that was in Seascape that would provide social continuity for Ian. After boarding the flight, Jim and I looked at Zillow, searching for options back in the neighborhood. One listing stood out. The home was completely remodeled with ocean views and separation of space so the boys could have privacy and their own living room. And it was only three blocks away. An energy climbed within, the known intuitive sensation I had come to rely on, and I felt a rightness. As we sat waiting for the plane to take off, I called a friend who was a realtor and asked to see the house upon our return. A week later, Jim put an offer on it, and a month later, we closed.

New love, new home, new hope.

Soon after getting settled in the new house, Connor announced he was moving to L.A. He planned on continuing his education at Santa Monica College, with the intent to transfer to the University of California. One of his closest friends was from L.A. and had recently returned there. I intuitively sensed Connor longed for independence and to begin living on his own terms. Since he had missed the traditional college experience, living away from home would provide him an essential bridge to adult life. I knew I would miss him terribly, for he remained the most resonant person in my life. I also knew that moving away was important for his growth. I wanted to unconditionally support that. Since he was a skilled surfer, he planned on becoming a surf instructor while taking a full load of classes. I was confident the move would be good for him, but knew it would hit Ian hard to have his brother no longer at home. I just didn't know at the time, despite my intuitive skills, that Ian was spiraling downward.

Jim and I were deeply enjoying our time together. We laughed a lot and were growing closer and stronger as a couple. We traveled a bit to connect away from the boys and occasionally I would accompany him to education industry conferences, no longer as a participant, rather as his girlfriend. We were an unlikely match.

"I have fallen in love with someone we used to work with," I confided in a former colleague, as we caught up over the phone. She and I had both reported to Jim back at McGraw-Hill, and I had known her since our time at Prentice Hall, early in our careers.

In response she quickly answered, "Well, I know who it *isn't*. No way it's Jim." On the outside, Jim and I were ill-suited for each other. He was reserved, conventional, sedentary, and didn't appear on the surface to be interested in personal growth or mystical experience. I had a rebellious spirit and had an outside-the-box reputation. Something about our differences created resonance. Jim felt a deep sense of mission to take care of me and to support my unrealized mission to be of service to others. I felt a sense of mission to help him become healthy and learn how to live.

I was not, however, ready yet for my mission. Unhealed layers of me became more visible as Ian became increasingly anxious and troubled. I knew in my heart that if it weren't for Jim providing for us, enabling me to be home everyday, I might have lost Ian forever. But instead I was there, holding the prayer, providing consistent presence, while not knowing at the time that my son was becoming a drug addict before my eyes.

Given that Connor was moving and I wanted to support him, I began to consider what work I could do from home that didn't require travel. Michael's finances continued to be thin, and I sensed it was important that I begin earning again. I didn't want Jim to pay for Connor's expenses, so I was determined to figure something out. I also knew that Ian needed me home. I prayed for a solution and quickly received one. My inner guidance was clear: *executive recruiting for the education industry*. Made a hell of a lot of sense. My career had created a network of trusted relationships that I could draw upon both to find clients as well as talent.

I began interviewing with a well-known search firm and had verbally accepted an offer. No papers were yet signed, as I had begun to feel a sense of wrongness about it. It felt a bit like *Glengarry Glen Ross*, a film that dramatized life in high-pressure sales, with incessant cold calling and obtrusive expectations. When the hiring manager talked about daily phone quotas, I immediately knew I couldn't do it. And as if by Divine providence, I soon learned that good, trusted friends of mine, whom I had known since the early days of my publishing career, were starting their own retained-search recruiting firm. I began talking with them and we quickly agreed that I would be part of it, though as an independent contractor. *Perfect!* I could make good money with no commute. I wanted most of me holding the home. I had found a solution that my heart could engage—working with people who were smart, full of integrity, and who I genuinely loved.

Two years after we moved into our new home, Jim and I married.

Jim had proposed to me on a trip to New York City as we sat on the same bar stools at Hurley's where he first proclaimed his love for me.

Our wedding had a fairy-tale quality about it. Barefoot, with only jewelry adorning my feet, my two sons walked me down the wooden stairs that led to the sand where my handsome, soon-to-be husband waited for me with such deep love in this eyes I could feel nothing but hope. The ocean had a Caribbean-teal color to it that day, as opposed to the greenish-grey you might expect from Monterey Bay. The weather was sunny and warm. Surrounded by dear friends and family, we shared our vows and cried as we gazed at each other with deep love and commitment.

Ironically, on the very spot we had reserved for our beach wedding, someone had sculpted a memorial to Wayne Dyer, who had just passed away. I wondered if removing the sand sculpture with his name carved on it with such care was an omen. Wayne had been one of my first spiritual teachers; the only concern that remained within me about marrying Jim was his lack of interest in spiritual growth. That concern would remain as the years unfolded. My question was, *How can you grow in the absence of a spiritual practice?* I chose to focus daily on feeling gratitude instead: gratitude for Jim's love, kindness, stability, and generosity. Not as a bypass to my concerns, rather as a conscious acknowledgement that gratitude for the life I was now living was the appropriate response. All relationships have their inherent challenges and differences, and my eyes were wide open about what I perceived ours to be.

While I would occasionally descend into some darkness about our union, most days I was happy and fulfilled in my marriage. But emotional intimacy was new for him. He hadn't experienced it in his first marriage, and his rather authoritarian father hadn't modeled for him the vulnerability needed for conscious union. On my dark days, I focused on what I perceived to be his lack of aliveness, his discomfort with emotional intimacy, and his failing health. In time I would finally realize that focusing on his perceived faults only widened the distance between us, and I was lonely enough as it was. I was never lonely while in meditation and prayer, for there was a depth and resonance to that union that felt like the home I had yet to experience but was committed to creating.

My focus now was on supporting Ian, who was adjusting to his new stepfather, another new school (he no longer needed explicit support for his dyslexia), and his brother's absence. His new school was not a good fit. They had hired three different math teachers in a matter of months, and the lack of consistency was affecting Ian's motivation. He was losing the sense that he could be successful. Given that he had just made such substantial progress, I did not want another school to leave a traumatic footprint, so we made a quick change. For the next year, I focused on supporting Ian in independent study. I would sit with him everyday, providing both emotional support as well as any other support he needed to get his work done. Ian was struggling with anxiety, seemed unable to focus most days, and I was increasingly concerned about his mental and emotional health. I was grateful that I could be home, focused on him and not much else. I was exactly where my son needed me to be. Our time together was creating a deep bond, a bond we would both need to help us through what was brewing under the surface.

Chapter 21. **Broken Open**

From the outside, all was well: a beautiful home, a stable, loving relationship with my husband, and a consistent presence for my Ian.

Maybe it was the contrast, the new stability, that accelerated the next wave of unraveling. Maybe my new marriage created unease, for Jim was so different than Michael. Or maybe too much pain and trauma remained unhealed. My hope that a stable home offering kindness, generosity, and consistency would be a salve for Ian began to seem inadequate. My sensitive Ian was like a canary in a coal mine. He would soon let me know that what had occurred in our past was coming home to roost. His sensitivity and depth was his super power, but at fifteen, he had no idea how to manage it. Instead, he just felt everything deeply, and most of what he felt had a despairing quality to it. While still at his previous school, Chartwell, he had written eloquently about himself in an assignment for the students to get to know each other and for the teachers to gain insights into their students. His poem was framed in the hallway of the school. I will never forget the moment I stopped to read it as I walked to my first teacher conference there. Ian had just turned twelve. I wept as I read.

Ian

I am an old soul who cares
I wonder of a place far, far away
I hear voices in my life
I see through the universe like it's glass
I want to know
I am an old soul who cares
I pretend to know the answer
I feel for lost people
I touch the end of time
I worry for the world
I cry for the world
I am an old soul who cares
I understand the universe
I say magical words
I dream of a dream
I try to understand
I hope for a better world
I am an old soul who cares

Our new home had a reversed floor plan, allowing for ocean views. What that also meant was that the kitchen was upstairs on the main level of the home, within earshot of the master bedroom. It was by hearing Ian's late-night snacking that I learned about his drug abuse.

I awoke one night to find him standing in the kitchen with his hand deep in the peanut butter jar, peanut butter smeared on his cheek and his eyes glazed over in a drug-induced stupor. He looked so unlike himself. He looked emaciated. He had always been thin, but this time was different—he looked pale, hollow. He was barely able to stand. As I got closer to him, he tried to carry on a conversation. I was devastated to see him so impaired, so lost, and clearly in so much emotional pain that the only choice he felt he had was to exit this life with drugs, to travel as far from the pain as he could.

I became vigilant each night, tracking his whereabouts on the iPhone and staying up to see with my own eyes the condition he was in. And most nights what I saw was my son greatly impaired. He would walk from the house to meet his "friends" in the neighborhood; their bond was drug use. I had an intense mix of emotions stirring within. Fear for his safety, anger at the many teachers who had failed him, intense frustration at how powerless I felt to help him, while also holding on to hope that somehow God would intervene and help my son. Months went by and with each passing day I was more depleted and gravely concerned about my son. I truly felt that it was possible something catastrophic could happen as the months dragged on. And I felt completely alone. Jim seemed ill-equipped to support me apart from his stated willingness to pay for rehab. With each passing day, Ian was becoming increasingly volatile. I needed a strong masculine presence to hold boundaries for Ian, but neither Michael nor Jim seemed able. Jim had a softness about him and a fear of confrontation. Michael was the opposite. He was often adversarial and, far from holding Divine masculine, more often than not what he held seemed toxic. I felt completely alone. I was losing vitality. I no longer felt like myself. Overcome with emotional exhaustion and constant worry, I prayed every day, sometimes every hour, hoping that my son would stop using, and I would feel emotionally supported in helping him find his way back, maybe for the first time, to health.

His addiction progressed. I decided, given that a year had passed and Ian was getting worse, I needed to find a residential solution, so I began searching online for a place where Ian could learn how to live sober. His father thought I was overreacting, even challenging my use of the word "addict." Perhaps it was because Michael used cannabis every day, as well as alcohol, that he couldn't abide my word choice. My search led me to a place in Marin, on the other side of the Golden Gate Bridge, that catered to young men and followed the 12-step program as the foundation for recovery. Jim generously agreed that, whatever the cost, he would pay for it. After he and I traveled to Marin to visit, I began to consider how to get Ian to agree to treatment.

I recognized that I was now at the lowest point of my life. While I had experienced great trauma and great transformation, witnessing the addiction of my teenaged son was the greatest pain I had yet known. My prayer and my connection to the Divine was all I felt I had to truly help me help my son. And it felt woefully inadequate. Part of me began to consider that my faith, my connection to Divine intelligence, was an illusion, for no matter how much I prayed, my son continued to spiral downward.

I think we have all heard the common wisdom that until someone hits bottom, nothing changes. I was certainly there, and now, looking back, Ian was getting close. My inner guidance insisted that rehab was not the solution, yet didn't illuminate what was—other than telling me to be patient, that, in time, Ian would heal. I was also told by my inner guidance not to punish him; that being punitive would only add to his despair and not address the underlying causes of his drug use. Ian was abusing anti-anxiety pills mostly, though I would learn years later that, other than heroine, he had tried almost everything else. He had befriended a man named Joey, many years older, who on the surface was charming and kind, yet I had an intuitive sense that he was a big part of my son's access to drugs. With no definitive proof, I sensed that Joey was Ian's supplier.

I was somewhat comforted for a time in Ian's willingness to go to therapy. He began seeing a therapist named Eric. When you confide in a therapist, should the therapist hear anything unlawful or consistent with child abuse, they must involve the authorities. Ian had shared a violent moment with his dad, just months after his 16th birthday, in which Michael, fed up with Ian's behavior, engaged in a physical altercation that bruised Ian's back. Eric responded to this story as he was legally bound to do, and now Child Protective Services was involved, investigating Michael for child abuse. Michael had not been physically abusive to Ian; one could easily argue that he had been defending himself from Ian's drug-induced aggression. And while I wished that Michael had handled himself differently, I empathized with Michael experiencing a breaking point. We were all fast approaching it. Our days were chaotic and frightening.

Connor had returned home to start his university education at University of California-Santa Cruz. While he had his pick of almost all the UCs, he chose to come home out of deep concern for his brother. He would often get in between Ian and me when Ian, seemingly out of his mind, would threaten me with physical violence. Ian was approaching bottom when a terrifying experience changed everything.

On a sunny afternoon in Michael's townhouse, where Ian was often unsupervised because Michael was either working or with his girlfriend, Ian witnessed his friend Joey overdose on heroin. Joey's heart stopped. Ian called 911. He held Joey in his arms as he waited for the paramedics to arrive and then watched as they resuscitated Joey, bringing him back to life.

That day, Ian proclaimed to himself that he would stop using. Rare is it that someone decides to stop using drugs without any professional intervention, but that is exactly what Ian did. He then went through the excruciating process of withdrawal as he courageously remained true to his inner commitment. I would hear him retching night after night as the vomiting served to clear his system. Once clean, he persisted in his commitment to stay sober. Soon he would excel in his remaining year in high school as he deepened his commitment to his health. His drive and his will were so inspiring to witness! What I am certain of is that Ian's determination to get healthy, coupled with a kind, stable, and prayer-filled home, provided the essential ingredients for his transformation. As the years unfolded, I would witness my son become confident, earn straight A's in college, become a certified personal trainer, and a counselor to his peers. The "old soul who cares" was finding his way, and I now I could commit to finding mine.

Chapter 22. Returning

With the freedom that came from a stable home and Ian's transformation, I began a conscious recommitment to myself, my healing, and to the mission that had been articulated to me the morning I had awakened, some twenty-five years earlier. Tucked away on the bottom shelves of my basement closet sat Rubbermaid containers housing pieces of myself: curricula I had written for the young people I had mentored post-awakening, notes I had taken when visiting with the founder of Forsyth School, my original Forsyth songbook, HeartMath guidebooks and presentations, and binders of articles I had collected that spoke to living consciously and healing with intention. I thought of my mother and her trunk, as she called it, that housed evidence of her extraordinary young life. Like her, I had collected pieces of wisdom, but then stored them away, not consciously thinking about them or caring for them. Yet they were patiently waiting for me, collecting dust, hopeful that one day I would return to them.

But the exhaustion that had overtaken my system while Ian had suffered lingered. I began looking for reasons beyond what I had just endured. I sensed there was more to it. My fatigue and lack of aliveness seemed to be trying to get my attention. I wondered what I needed to do to feel better. I often thought it was Jim— that somehow he was affecting the zest for life I had felt before he became my partner. He was so still and quiet. Living in someone else's energy field has consequences. *Could it be that?* I sought out psychics and healers, yet no revelation emerged. Though one psychic did ask me as soon as he emerged from wherever he traveled to receive his psychic messages, "So, when are you going to write your book?"

In my quest to understand why I felt so unlike myself, I would continue to blame menopause referencing the lists of symptoms that reflected how I felt. *Maybe all women in their fifties feel this way?*

I decided, with the encouragement of my intuition, that the best way to feel better would be to immerse myself in what I had known, what I had learned, and most importantly, how I had felt the day I awakened.

Every morning, after making a cup of coffee, I would find a quiet place to meditate and pray. I would consciously re-experience how I felt when I first opened my eyes in bed in my San Francisco hotel suite, tapping into that energy. Recreating it as best I could each morning, started to turn on dormant gifts. I opened the Rubbermaid containers and got reacquainted with their contents. I voraciously reread my favorite spiritual books, studying *A Course in Miracles* again, trying to bring a beginner's mind to it all. Given that all I had known and learned hadn't yet been consistently reflected in my circumstances, studying it all again with the intent of staying disciplined was long overdue. I was gradually coming back to life. I felt more intuitive, more connected to Divine intelligence. I deepened my time in heart-centered meditation. Jim and I were doing well together and were both enjoying the new ease that was present. I recognized that it was unfair to expect Jim to check all my boxes—what he provided me was more than enough to live a good, fulfilling life. I could find my spiritual tribe—or create one—and that could be separate from my life at home. He showed up in my life as if he had a spiritual practice. He was stable and kind, a generous soul, and a beautiful lover. *For God's sake, Regan, have that be enough*!

My immersion in my spiritual study was helping me access more vitality, but I still felt tired. For at least twenty years, I had done high-impact aerobics almost daily. And now I simply didn't have the energy for it, so I asked in prayer what I should do instead. And I quickly received: *yoga*.

I had practiced yoga on and off for years but never with any real commitment or consistency. Message received, I began taking classes at a beautiful yoga studio in Capitola not far from our house. The quality of instruction there and the practice itself was soothing to my soul while strengthening my body. Something was shifting. I was softening. I was healing, yet again. I became more disciplined in my practice and met new friends at the studio that felt like resonant reflections of me.

Ian began taking classes at the local community college, just as his brother had done. Connor had graduated from University of California-Santa Cruz with a degree in English Literature and had started working at Soif—the elegant wine bar where I had celebrated my 44th birthday—helping to manage their retail space. Living with friends, Connor seemed to be enjoying his life and the community of new friends he had made through work.

For the first time in a very long time, I felt ease with the freedom to again be a student of spiritual science. The owner of the studio and I became good friends. We felt deep resonance and ease when we were together. Like me, she was highly intuitive. One day at the studio we decided that it would be rewarding and fun to teach classes together, so for the next few months we met regularly and created a curriculum that reflected what we knew and what we wanted to share with the community. We named the series "Ready to Awaken." It was, in some ways, a deconstruction of my spiritual awakening coupled with an orientation to spiritual principles that we tried earnestly to live by. We hoped that the deep work that our curriculum reflected would be an agent of healing and transformation for our students. Finding a committed group to teach came easily, and I was feeling deep fulfillment in how I was spending my time.

In meditation one day, I was told to pursue yoga teacher training. My favorite local teacher was promoting her 200-hour training, held at the yoga studio where I was teaching my Ready to Awaken course. The inner resonance I felt upon hearing the inner guidance, the call to be a yoga teacher, was deep and wide. *How funny*, I thought, *given that I started my life practicing Tai Chi and meditation daily, that it is just now occurring to me to teach yoga.* The rightness of it was crystal clear, and my husband's emotional and financial support immediate. I began reading the Yoga Sutras, the Upanishads, and the Bhagavad Gita in preparation, books I had never read previously.

Funny how when life had an easy cycle it seemed to be quickly followed by a not-so-easy cycle. I wondered if that was just the nature of life, cycles of ease then complexity, for even the rhythm of the heart was a pattern of acceleration (sympathetic-nervous-system activation) followed by a slowing down (parasympathetic-nervous-system activation). Or was it somehow a reflection of the polarity that had colored my childhood? Whatever the reason, just as ease and flow was becoming the norm, with my newly earned yoga teacher training certification in hand, we began to hear of this highly contagious flu-like bug that was killing people in Italy. With its origins in China, now it was sickening people in New York City.

The pandemic was beginning and everything would soon dramatically change. Gavin Newsom and his "progressive" policies would have those of us in California locked down for over a year. Thank God we had a stable foundation to hold us as the world went mad.

Chapter 23. Madness

I have often wondered if we all, as a collective, didn't fear death, what would life be like? Would our priorities change? Would we take more risks? Would we have more fun?

As the pandemic evolved, that question was in the forefront of my mind and heart. Outdoor playgrounds covered in yellow caution tape preventing their use, sand poured into skate parks so children couldn't skate, police with assault weapons in hand escorting people off public beaches, arrows pointing where to walk in grocery stores, faces masks and hand sanitizer everywhere, signs warning you to keep six feet apart, children not able to play in public spaces, teachers from elementary school through university forced to move classes online with no training. Nothing made logical or intuitive sense. People were terrified and what they feared was death.

A few months after the Covid lockdowns began, I had a direct experience with what felt like dark energy. A lightning storm raged on a warm August night, the skies were lit up. For reasons I have never understood, in the Bay Area we hardly ever have lightning or thunderstorms. I am sure someone could explain why, but I had just accepted that, for whatever reason, California storms are just rain.

But this night was different. Massive lightning marked the skies. As I watched, the energy felt ominous, not natural. Just like throwing a lit matchstick on dry grass, my beloved Santa Cruz mountains began to rage in flames. I had first fallen in love with the mountains when I moved to work at HeartMath, and then over time I met kind people with a love for music and nature who tried to live in conscious harmony with the majestic trees and rolling hills of the range. One of my closest friends, Nicole, was almost religious in her tending to her land, providing biodynamic preparations each season to keep her soil nourished and enlivened. She hosted beautiful gatherings as we sang under the stars, the canopy of the redwoods and pines protecting us in a deep hug.

As the winds picked up, even though the fires were over thirty miles from my home, my car was covered in big flakes of ash. The skies had a menacing feel and look to them, choked off with smoke as the fire was stoked by increasing wind. Then evacuations were ordered, and some of my closest friends were running for their lives. In the middle of the night, Nicole came to my home, exhausted and panicked, bringing only her two dogs, having left her beloved goats and cat behind. I was so relieved when I saw her at my front door; I hugged her for as long as she would let me. At least she was safe. That night, almost 1,000 homes burned to ash and most of my tribe on the mountain lost everything. It didn't feel right. The energy of it felt manmade, somehow. And while I will never know for certain what caused the fires, I do trust my inner sight, which told me it was an act of violence and what underlay it was a desire for people to be forced from remote living to more populated areas where they could be more easily controlled.

Fast forward seven months and control, for our "safety," was the norm. I drove with my husband so he could get the Covid vaccine, which was touted as "safe and effective." Government, medical, and civil leadership, and media personalities shouted that if you were vaccinated, you wouldn't get or spread the virus. While

I wasn't completely clear at first about it, my inner guidance, the voices I trusted, were clear: *Do not get vaccinated.* And so I didn't. I also believed in choice. If people wanted to get it, I wasn't going to convince them otherwise; people should choose what they inject in their bodies. It is not my role to convince them of anything.

But mandatory vaccination soon became public policy. If you wanted to work, go to school, or deliver healthcare, you were required to get the Covid vaccine. How could a vaccine, which usually takes ten years to develop, become available in less than twelve months? How could any public health agency claim it was safe, given that little time had elapsed to truly understand if that was true? How could the nightly news provide daily counts of death when typically in takes weeks for death certificates to be processed? Again, nothing felt like it made any sense—logically or intuitively. A social bifurcation resulted. If you were unvaxxed, you were perceived as a threat to global health. Polls showed that people had no problem fining the unvaxxed, denying them healthcare or access to public spaces. I began to live what felt like a dystopian nightmare. Even my closest friend raged at me for not getting vaccinated. People were so afraid to die and their fear had them losing their humanity and their critical thinking.

"I WANT YOU TO DIE!" screamed a woman at my friends and me as we walked the Presidio in San Francisco after marching peacefully in protest of the mandatory vaccine. I carried a sign that read, "When there is risk, there must be choice." Any vaccine, much less one developed almost overnight, has risks—just read the package insert: it names them all in black and white. The protest had attracted people from across the Bay Area and the resultant congestion near the protest site had traffic stopped and drivers clearly pissed. As we walked, carrying our signs, trying to catch an Uber back to our car, the rage we encountered was frightening. I told the group that, for our safety, we should dispose of our signs. We did so, and continued walking. As the walk dragged on for over an hour, my heartburn was intense and I was having trouble staying with the group. I paused and said a prayer asking for help. I simply couldn't walk anymore. As I continued to pray, a small bus appeared, seemingly out of nowhere. I flagged it down. "Could you please give us a ride to the edge of the Presidio? I am exhausted." The driver kindly agreed. The few military residents he was driving didn't mind the favor, and I felt deeply grateful that my prayer was so quickly answered. As we rested in the bus, I reflected on the rage I had just witnessed. *How could strangers want me dead just because I was peacefully protesting a mandatory vaccine?* Fear has people do unspeakable things. I had certainly lived that as a child. Now, as a middle-aged adult, I was seeing the same kind of rage in the eyes of strangers.

Now, in 2023, we know that the vaccine is not safe and not effective. And while forces are still trying very hard to silence dissent, the data is clear. The Covid vaccine does not prevent illness or transmission. Data doesn't lie. And brave voices like the CEO of the OneAmerica insurance company publicly disclosed that during the third and fourth quarters of 2021, death in people of working age (18–64) was 40 percent higher than it was before the pandemic. Significantly, the majority of the deaths were not attributed in any way to Covid. Ed Dowd, former analyst for Blackrock, renowned expert on making sense of data to inform investment decisions on Wall Street, began sounding the alarm as a result of the data. From February 2021 to March 2022, millennials experienced more than 60,000 excess deaths. His groundbreaking book *Cause Unknown: The Epidemic of Sudden Deaths in 2021 & 2022* is a wake-up call for anyone interested in the truth. I will leave it to you to draw your own conclusions.

In contrast to the literal insanity of life on the outside, our home was a kind, safe haven. I ordered paint-by-numbers online and would spend hours a day painting, which helped pass the time. And while I tired of cooking, I was consciously grateful that we all were safe and had the resources needed to carry on with relative ease. Jim no longer worked at the office and spent his workday in the main living space of the home, going from one Zoom meeting to the next. Unfortunately our home wasn't well designed for pandemic working. Jim didn't have an office in the house; all the bedrooms were accounted for, so he worked in the living room. After a year of this, we all were fatigued. Who wants to hear someone work all day long? I longed for my own space too, where I could pray and meditate without interruption. I kidded Jim that I needed a she shed—a space where I could pray, meditate, reflect, and listen. Outdoor spaces were still monitored. I craved space. I would go downstairs to Connor's bedroom to try to sustain my spiritual practice, which just before Covid, was constant and deeply nourishing. I was becoming less disciplined due to circumstances, and I was aware that I didn't feel well. I had what felt like constant heartburn. As I regularly referred to the list of symptoms for menopause, I could see heartburn clearly delineated—a top-five symptom. I thought little of it, even though my symptoms were often intense, though I was curious why Tums never helped ease the pain.

To express my gratitude to Jim's boss, who was treating his employees with great care, I offered to teach yoga online for the employees as an act of service. I knew pandemic stress was real. People were isolated and afraid. People were prevented from seeing their sick family members. People were dying alone without the comfort of loving touch or a loving gaze. I hoped that preparing my class each week would encourage me to stay disciplined in my practice and provide much-needed teaching experience. Even though Zoom was easy to use, it felt a bit awkward to share yoga over the internet. The spiritual intimacy was easier to create when together in a studio space. But in times of crisis, it is helpful to be flexible. I was trying. I sought refuge traveling by car, housesitting or staying in Airbnbs to get away and to begin writing my story. I had decided to at least begin. I headed first to Nevada City to see a dear friend, to hold ceremony for my ancestors, and hopefully gain some insights that would propel me to write.

But Ian was struggling in his online classes, now the Covid norm; his teachers clearly had no interest in actually delivering instruction. Instead they quickly packaged their courses in modules where he was told to read module one, take a quiz, repeat. It reminded me of the correspondence courses in the '80s—the only difference was the internet delivered the content as opposed to the U.S. mail. Ian loved to learn, but he wasn't interested in teaching himself general education courses like sociology, English composition, and algebra. Online college wasn't working for him; he was losing enthusiasm. When the lockdowns ended, if you wanted to return to class face-to-face, you were required to have the Covid vaccine. Ian didn't want that, and God knows I didn't want that for him, so he dropped out, hoping that the rules, in time, would change.

How my community responded to the pandemic changed everything for me. What I had perceived as a conscious, spiritual community no longer felt that way—instead it felt as if the spiritual focus of my community was actually just another response to fear. People who understand their divinity, who truly understand that they are eternal, do not behave as I had witnessed. I felt very alone. And while I had made a few new, deep connections with people who shared my intuitive sense about the pandemic and the vaccine, I no longer felt like I belonged in Santa Cruz. I would often look at Zillow, seeing what money could buy in other places across the country. And in that search, I would occasionally look at my hometown of St. Louis, feeling somewhat curious about what life could be like back where it began. What I was clear about was the importance of writing my story. I had healed so much. I had finally attracted a stable, well-resourced life. I had a kind, loving, consistent partner. I had returned to myself. I had recommitted to my spiritual practice, even though the lockdowns and the lack of privacy challenged it! I felt very close to God and to my guides, whose voices I could hear more clearly. I was committed to figuring out what was in my highest good to do.

In sensing that, I could also sense that change was coming. Funny thing about my intuition: the biggest events in my life, I never see coming. I am grateful that this is true, for it keeps the mystery alive and enables more growth by having to adapt to ever-evolving circumstances without being shown what was coming or how it would resolve. I didn't see Jim coming. I didn't sense I was pregnant with Ian. And what was soon to be the greatest transformative circumstance of my life was not in my awareness either.

Chapter 24. **Heeding the Call**

Seeking refuge, renewal, and some much needed privacy, in early December of 2021, I headed to Joshua Tree, an hour or so outside of Palm Springs. I was drawn to its beauty and its potent energy. For centuries, indigenous people viewed the land as highly sacred, a place to connect to strength and resilience. I arrived at my Airbnb with the intention to continue writing and renew my spirit, which I felt was dragging from the collective Covid fear. Each time I wrote, I would begin first in prayer and meditation. "Sweet loving spirit, angels of love and of light, my guides, ancestors of the highest vibration and intention, I ask you to be with me. Guide my voice so that my writing is an agent of the highest good. Help me to remember. Help me be an agent of healing and transformation for myself and my readers."

After speaking aloud my prayer, I became still. Anchoring my focus in my heart, directing the inhales and exhales there, coming into an easeful rhythm of breath. Once I felt present in my heart through the breath, I recalled the morning I awakened. I activated all my senses as I remembered, but most importantly, I remembered how I felt. *The infinite calm. The infinite knowing. The limitless love and compassion. The wisdom. The hope.* I soaked in that feeling as deeply as I could and, if my mind began to chat, as is its nature, I refocused in the heart and reconnected to the energy of my awakening. I become highly receptive to my inner guidance. I listened. I sat.

You must urgently move back home.

That inner voice that I had known so well that day spoke with an urgency that was different. Not panicked, but urgent. The voice said nothing more. This was the same voice I had come to rely on, and I knew in my heart the truth of what it compelled. So I came out of meditation, found my cell phone, and called an old, dear friend who had recently changed careers to become a real estate agent in St. Louis. "Andrea, I just came out of prayer and meditation. I'm in Joshua Tree working on a book. I was just told by a trusted inner voice that I need to urgently move home. I have no idea why, but I have learned to do as my Spirit tells me. I plan on flying out of Palm Springs in the morning. Would you please work with me so I can find a new home? I know it sounds dramatic, but can you help me?" She immediately agreed and would pick me up at the airport so we could begin our search. I then called Jim and told him what I had just been told. Without hesitation, he offered his support and made the airline reservations using airline points. He had no questions for me, just unconditional love, "If that is what you are being told, then, of course."

I had seen a listing on Zillow that piqued my interest a few months prior: a historic home on a few acres that also housed a chapel and a banquet facility. It was a wedding venue that I thought could be easily converted into our home but could also serve as a spiritual retreat center. No rational thinking was operating. I was just doing as I was being directed. I hadn't thought since my late twenties about having a spiritual center, but suddenly I was seeing that whatever was next included teaching and sharing publicly what I had come to understand. Yet before I even had left for the airport, I knew that property wasn't it. So I just kept praying, asking for the highest good to be made manifest and to find where I was supposed to be.

Andrea and I drove to the north side of St. Louis to see the wedding venue. And while the property was stunning, even considering where in town it was, I knew it wasn't where I was supposed to be. She and I decided to grab some dinner to spend time looking again at the MLS. Nothing resonated. I continued to silently pray to be directed to the right place. "Why don't we broaden our search to include Franklin County?" As the words came out of my mouth, I felt I wasn't speaking them. I wasn't even sure where Franklin County was, other than I vaguely remembered it was the county that housed my Dad's estate years ago. Andrea began to look. And then I saw it.

A gorgeous home, housed on ten acres, with what looked like a man cave—a large building, about fifty yards from the house, made with the same brick and stone, with three large, dramatic garage doors. The photos of the interior of the building showcased a couple of tractors, a pool table, a sectional facing an enormous television, ceilings that looked to be at least fifteen feet high, and a disco ball hanging from the ceiling in the center of the 2,800-square-foot space. *Now, that's a large man cave! Can I convert this into a place where I can teach and retreat?*

I really wanted our new home to have its own water source. Living through a drought in California with $400 water bills inspired me to want our own, and I sensed that in the future, access to water would matter—a lot. But while the MLS description didn't include mention of a well, it was still a compelling property that warranted a visit. I told Andrea I wanted to see it, so she quickly got on the phone to make arrangements. I heard her say to the listing agent, "I have a California buyer who wants to see the listing on Cardinal Meadows before she heads back tomorrow night. Would that be possible?" The phrase "California buyer" comes with the perception of money, given the prices we pay for homes there, so in a matter of minutes Andrea had arranged for us to visit the next morning. I had a really good feeling about it, though I had no idea where Washington, Missouri, was, or what kind of town I would find there.

In the morning, Andrea and I drove down Interstate 44 for about an hour, heading west from St. Louis. As we drove, I googled "Washington, Missouri." The photos of the downtown were quaint, exuding small-town charm, churches with dramatic architecture, and small businesses standing with pride on the banks of the Missouri River. Washington looked like a sweet small town with a focus on Jesus and family. I had a feeling of hope and excitement as we entered the neighborhood. Gorgeous homes stood back far from the road, massive lawns, manicured with care. I imagined how beautiful the trees and expansive lots would look come spring. We parked in front of the house and the energy felt wonderful. Beautifully maintained, the home had a regal sense about it. As I took it all in, I felt a warm excitement. A man, who I assumed was the owner, came quickly up the driveway in a golf cart with a beaming smile and welcoming manner. Before I even said a word, he—unprompted—exclaimed, "Well hello, young lady. I should mention we have a geothermal well here." It was as if God was speaking to me. Before heading inside, I knew I had found home.

After touring, Andrea and I ventured to the historic downtown for lunch. As we came down Jefferson Street, heading towards the river, my eyes were drawn to a building that sat on the corner. In etched writing on the windows it read, "Blu Room. UVB Light & Sound Therapy. Reiki. Massage." I gazed down the street to see another sign, "Present Moment Yoga." The Divine was letting me know that I would find resonance in this rural town, where yard signs read "I trust in Jesus" with light emanating from Jesus' heart. I marveled at how many homes we drove past had signs exclaiming their love and trust in Jesus. Yet somehow, in this little town, there was also an appetite for innovative light and sound therapy, energy healing, and yoga. I was comforted at all of these signs from beyond that I was where I was supposed to be.

"Honey, I know I have found our new home. Gorgeous house, a finished lower level with its own kitchen and entrance for Ian, ten wooded acres, beautifully grand windows, a geothermal well, a big hot tub off the master bedroom deck, and a 2,800-square-foot man cave/garage that we could convert into a center. Look on Zillow. I absolutely love it!" I had been kidding that God wanted me to open a "come work on your shit" center. I would find that that description was readily understood. If I said "spiritual enrichment center," people's eyes would glaze over. Sight unseen, Jim put an offer on the house a few days after I returned from my dramatic house-hunting trip. He knew I was following the urgent guidance of the Holy Spirit. Jim wanted nothing more than to support what Spirit was directing, so we began the work to put our beach house on the market and get ready for the most important move of our lives.

The week our beach house was listed, we received multiple cash offers. My dear friends planned a going away party. I had spent almost twenty-five years in Santa Cruz, yet there would only be a few people I would truly miss. I also knew that those I would miss would remain in my life. A long arduous chapter of life seemed to be coming to a close. I reflected deeply on all of it and as I prepared to move. I visited each home I had lived in, to offer my prayer and to get more deeply in touch with who I was in each place, what I had learned, how I had grown through the joy and pain of the life I had led. I took comfort in a poem written by Emory Hall that fit so well how I felt as I blessed each California address:

> make peace
> with all the women
> you once were.
> lay flowers at their feet.
> offer them incense
> and honey

and forgiveness.
honor them
and give them your silence.
listen.
bless them
and let them be.
for they are the bones
of the temple
you sit in now.
for they are the rivers of wisdom
leading you toward
the sea.
I have been a thousand different women

Ian thought I had lost my mind; having lived only in Santa Cruz, he strongly resisted the move. I understood his point of view. I told him he had agency. If he didn't want to live in Missouri, he could find a way back to Santa Cruz through hard work and savings. I sensed that this move would be a turning point for Ian. I had felt for sometime that he was continually triggered by living in the same neighborhood where he had been an addict. My intuition told me he would find greater health and wellbeing in Missouri. I trusted in time he would see that too. I explained that I had been urgently told by my inner guidance to move. He questioned who my guidance was—why would they say that? I validated his concerns but stood firm in my knowing.

The only person I struggled to leave was my son Connor. Connor had a new girlfriend he was excited about and spent a lot of his free time drinking with his tribe, all of whom worked in restaurants downtown. Anthony Bourdain was right: the restaurant world seemed to be filled with people with substance issues. I often wondered if Connor was okay.

Since our move was imminent, I had as many family dinners as possible, wanting to see Connor as much as I could. If it weren't for the inner voice telling me the move was necessary, I would have felt more conflicted to leave my twenty-seven-year-old son. Since Connor's father had moved back to St. Louis a year or so before, it meant that Connor's whole family would now be residing in Missouri. I trusted that if he felt drawn to move back to the place where he was born, he would. All I knew was that I was doing as God directed.

A few weeks before we were scheduled to move, Connor came over for dinner. He rummaged through his room one last time, gathering what he wanted and showing me what he wanted me to take with us to Missouri—mostly hundreds of his books. He seemed agitated and vacant and was drinking. I don't remember what he and Ian began quarreling about—I couldn't hear them as I cleaned up the kitchen—but it got intense. Then Connor stormed out of the house. I followed. As we stood there, a little boy who lived across the street came running to me, crying, saying his mother was gone and he didn't know where she was. I held him and reassured him that I would find his mother. As I grabbed my phone to call the boy's mother in one hand while holding close the terrified boy with the other, Connor remained by my side. I took a big exhale when the mother answered her phone, explaining that she had left the house to run a quick errand. I shared the news with the little boy as he continued to weep in my arms. I then looked up at Connor who was overcome with emotion, his raging eyes filled with tears. And as I did, Connor looked at me intensely and said, "I was sexually abused when I was little, Mom." And Ian, unbeknownst to me, with his unconscious psychic access, had named the perpetrator to Connor moments before, prompting Connor to storm out. I had no idea what to do or say. I just stood there taking it in as Connor shared that his repressed memories had been bubbling up for days. Something about the scared little boy I was holding, who was the same age as Connor when he was abused, created the conditions for Connor to feel with certainty the truth of what he had endured. My heart broke. *How the hell am I going to now move away with my beloved son torn apart by this horrendous remembrance?* All I could do was pray. Pray for the highest good. Pray to be directed as God willed.

Connor became increasingly unstable and continued drinking heavily. He filed a police report, a conscious act to do something to help him feel in control. He called me after he had filed, and I knew he was at a true crisis point. He was raging, sounding manic on the phone as I sped towards the house he was renting with friends. As I arrived, Connor was drinking a beer. It was 10:00 am. After I gave him a deep, long hug, I gazed in his soulful eyes and said, "You need help. You can't drink your way out of this. I am concerned about your health and safety."

He gazed back at me with a surrendered wisdom. "Yes, Mom. I agree. I need help."

With focused urgency, I began Googling residential treatment facilities where Connor could process his trauma and learn how to live without alcohol. Connor admitted he was an alcoholic and, within the hour, he had spoken to someone at Serenity Knolls, a facility in Marin highly rated for their approach to treating addiction and the trauma that underlies it. Jim knew it all, and as I called him to tell him that Connor had agreed to rehab, he generously shared, "Whatever it takes to get Connor help." In this case, "help" looked like over $35,000. Connor had minimal health insurance, so we needed to pay cash. Another vital moment where Jim's love and generosity shined brightly, without conditions or hesitation. Twenty-four hours later, Connor was safe at Serenity Knolls where he would be a resident for the next thirty days.

My heart ached, but I was deeply relieved knowing that he would at least be safe there. He would need to have a medically supervised detox. And I was scheduled to move two thousand miles away, two weeks later. What I also knew was that Connor's healing was something only he could do. I sensed that not being close to him was actually in his best interest. He would need to rely on himself, not me, if he was going to learn how to be and stay sober.

Connor made a dramatic entrance as he entered the facility. I have no idea how much he drank that morning. An hour or so after arriving, Connor lost consciousness. They called 911 and the paramedics came in minutes to revive him. As he came to, they told me he stood up, ripped his shirt off, revealing his various tattoos, and yelled. "I am back. I am the second coming!" He was then put in an ambulance and taken to the ER where they would run a number of blood tests, all of which were normal. Even though he had been binge-drinking for weeks, there was nothing physiologically wrong. A miracle, really. I fielded a call from the resident psychiatrist the following day who shared his concerns about their ability to help him. Given his dramatic behavior, they thought he was psychotic.

I then told the psychiatrist about my history. My dramatic awakening. The entities I saw. The voices I heard. I was lucid and clear as I explained that in the 12 Steps, the very program that was the foundation of their recovery approach, it names surrendering to a higher power as essential to recovery. Then calmly, with as much love as I could offer, I told the psychiatrist that most have truly no idea what that means. That it isn't an abstract notion; rather it is a very concrete reality. Connor, like me, had many paranormal experiences, and like me, there wasn't anything crazy about him. Rather, he was connected to the Divine in ways he was still making sense of and his remembering being sexually abused had him not in his right mind.

Whatever I said, he agreed to let him remain in their care. Two weeks later, Connor was a model resident, offering support to his peers and deep, wise, divinely inspired reflections as he sat in small groups processing his trauma and learning how to commit to sobriety.

Now, almost two years later, Connor remains sober. His girlfriend is now his partner. They live in Silicon Valley, creating a conscious and intimate life together.

As Connor was in treatment, I still felt conflicted about leaving him but I knew in my heart that moving back to Missouri, to an inspiring home that had the infrastructure for me to serve my community in my unique way, was exactly what God wanted me to do.

Chapter 25. Broken Heart

As I packed my suitcase, I felt deep peace and connection to the Divine. I contemplated what clothes and other items would carry me through the next couple of weeks as the moving truck made its way across the country. We had negotiated buying some furniture from the owners of our new home; it was a much larger home than the one we had sold. I was grateful to have beds and a few chairs when we arrived. I was going to fly to St. Louis with our recently adopted feral cat. Jim was going to stay behind for a week or so to attend to a few transactional details with the sale. And Ian was road-tripping with his father, who had flown back to California so they could drive east together, hiking the Grand Canyon along the way. Ian was excited for time with his dad. I was grateful that they would be having quality time in nature, a place where they both thrived.

My only concern was the cat. He had a fiery spirit. I consulted with the vet to help me understand how to help him adapt to the new place. He needed to stay inside for two months, which I knew he was going to not like, for he enjoyed his days outside, hunting mice and feeling the freedom of outdoor living. The vet gave me drugs to administer before the flight so he would feel relaxed. I chuckled when my guides told me he was going to become mostly an indoor cat in Missouri; I found that highly improbable, yet they had been right about everything else to date.

But I continued to feel tired as my heartburn raged. I had accepted it as a symptom of menopause. Before I flew to my new life, I wanted to experience as much of the Santa Cruz that I loved as I could. I walked West Cliff Drive with a grateful heart, the jagged cliffs framing my way. I continued to reflect on the lessons, the joys, and the heartaches of the life I was leaving. I ate at all my favorite restaurants, savored my kale smoothies, and practiced at all my favorite yoga studios. I was ready. I was also conscious, as I practiced yoga and walked, that I was out of shape. Crediting my lack of fitness to the sedentary lifestyle during the lockdowns, I was eager to get back into shape—though I wondered how I was going to do that given my lack of energy. I committed to myself that one of my priorities, once we were settled, was to get back into shape. I visualized working out at a new gym and meeting new friends who were also prioritizing their health.

My cat and I arrived at our new home the evening of March 28, 2022. I marveled at the stars, so visible in the night sky, not masked by city lights. The land spoke to me. I felt it was welcoming me with its loving wisdom. My best friend, Heidi—the same friend who had helped me survive the chaos and trauma of my childhood—made a couple of weeks' worth of meals to ease the transition. I was excited to be back near her. While I had been gone almost twenty-five years, we were as close as ever. She met me at the new house, gave me a big, best-friend hug, and we shared a toast to my following Spirit's direction as we affirmed our love and excitement for living close to one another again.

As I tried to sleep that night, my cat was highly distressed, meowing, moaning really, as I tried to sleep. I looked up what was best to do and locked him away in the laundry room, where the small space might comfort him and lessen his overwhelm. We both could finally rest.

We were slowly adjusting to our new reality. My heart was full of hope, the kind that comes when you begin something new. I walked my land with intention, praying as I walked, introducing myself to the spirits of the land, and asking for their help in bringing my vision to life. Once Jim and Ian arrived, we celebrated the new place. Ian loved it and even allowed some enthusiasm to shine through. We felt alive as a family as we sat in the hot tub with its inspiring view of the land. At night, the skies were so majestic I wanted to learn more about the constellations that held us, for I had forgotten what I'd known about them. While we had neighbors, the ten acres made us feel as if we lived alone. I loved having neighbors, but not seeing them.

As the days went by, a clear sense of rightness filled me. I was sure we were where God wanted us to be. Connor was transitioning well from rehab to a sober life. We offered to support him fully for a few months so he could ease back into his working life. He needed to find new work away from alcohol and our support helped ease the time pressure so he could focus on his health. What mattered most was his commitment to his sobriety, and I wanted him to focus solely on that. Connor was stable. I could exhale.

Then, in prayer and meditation each day, I began to receive information. I saw the remodel design of the man cave-garage in my mind, how it was going to feel, and what I was to offer there once it was ready.

I learned of a Facebook group called "What's Up Wash MO!" and I began to promote a free yoga class on my lawn. I was directed by my guides not to charge for yoga; I was told that, in time, the practice would encourage those who attended to be more curious about how to live a healthy and conscious life. I expected a rather tepid response to my Facebook post offering, so I was shocked to see over 250 people respond. Perhaps there was a true need for what Spirit was directing me to offer. I was told that, in addition to yoga, I should offer spiritual coaching, teaching HeartMath, and sharing my Ready to Awaken courses. I was making the inner plans while finding a contractor to execute my vision. And slowly, the man cave that reeked of cigarettes and cigars transformed into a yoga center. I began connecting with others interested in the healing arts. Clearly Spirit was leading the way, making the social transition easy. I began going to the Blu Room, which had served as a reassuring symbol during my first visit that I could find resonance here. The owner, Sara, and I felt like it was an ancient reunion when we first met. I had a sense that she and I would not only become close friends, but also collaborators. I loved walking along the river. The only thing missing was organic food and conscious places to eat.

Construction began. Ian was slowly accepting his new home. One day he admitted, "You know, Mom, the energy here feels a lot better." He would explore the woods during the day and sit outside at night, taking in the peaceful vibe that was easily felt.

Now late June, I was excited to get to know my surroundings, explore the countryside, and continue to get to know my new community. My commitment to my spiritual practices was very much alive within me; I spent hours a day praying and meditating to be shown the way forward. I affirmed everyday my commitment to be of service and asked that the insights, resources, and people come forth to enable me to serve.

Then, one fate-filled day in meditation, a new message came through.

"You need to go to the doctor."

The voice was firm and crystal clear. There was an uncompromising quality to the message. I typically don't go to Western doctors because their focus is rarely on healing the root causes of disease. Their solution too often, is pharmaceutical drugs, which doesn't make sense to me. I did do routine screenings, was fairly consistent about getting pap smears, and had learned years ago that I had a bicuspid aortic valve, a congenital heart defect, but I never really gave that any thought. In fact, I never thought about it at all.

But within a few minutes after receiving the message, I had found a local doctor with five stars—Craig Holzem—and made an appointment to see him a few days later. Other than honoring my guidance, as I had learned to do over my life, which always felt reassuring, I felt and sensed no fear or trepidation. No sense of what was coming.

I arrived early to Dr. Holzem's to fill out the substantial paperwork that comes with being a new patient. When asked in the paperwork about my health history, family history, and my reason for the appointment, I didn't write, "I am here because the Holy Spirit told me to be," but that was the truth. I wrote that I wanted to establish care with a new doctor since I was new to the area. I am not sure if I even remembered to list my bicuspid aortic valve issue, that's how faint it was in my awareness. The only medical events I had experienced were getting my tonsils out at age nine and childbirth.

Adorned on the walls of the room they asked me to wait in were spectacular, evocative photographs of people from across the world. The faces exuded such depth. I could sense the life they had lived from their eyes. When the doctor walked in, I shared with him my love of the photos. He shared that had taken them over time as he traveled the world. I liked him. He then listened to my heart, as doctors do, and almost immediately looked gravely concerned. "You have a significant, loud murmur. I need to get you scheduled for an echocardiogram as soon as possible."

"What is an echocardiogram?" I naively asked.

He explained it was the most efficient, non-invasive way to look at the heart and know how it is functioning. We then spoke briefly about my bicuspid valve, and he immediately thought that what he was hearing was the defective valve. I wasn't afraid, just curious about where this unexpected development was leading.

The echocardiogram was scheduled for the next day. Dr. Holzem was clearly concerned. Jim drove me to the local hospital where I would lie down for forty-five minutes while the technician took a detailed picture of my heart. She seemed a little confused at one point, and I asked her what she was seeing. She quickly replied that she couldn't say anything. I would need to wait until a cardiologist reviewed the images. That didn't feel good. I sensed she was afraid about what she saw. As I lay there, I continued to hold my prayer, as I always did, asking for the highest good to be made manifest, to bring me the resources, insights, and people needed for me to live my highest blueprint and to serve as an agent of the highest good.

I was beginning to sense that something significant was happening.

The following day, I quickly picked up the phone as it rang, seeing Esse Health, the name of my doctor's group, across the screen. In the next few minutes, I would learn that my aortic valve was highly calcified from having had to work so hard, given its congenital issue. Dr. Holzem did reassure me that I had a high ejection fraction—in other words, my heart was able to pump a higher-than-normal amount of blood with each contraction. He told me that I needed to confer quickly with a heart surgeon to learn from an expert what intervention was needed. I immediately thought of Barnes Hospital back in St. Louis where I was born, where my first son was born, and where I comforted my father when he was treated there for lung cancer. I wasn't comfortable seeking treatment in my rural town so instead of pursuing the referral that my doctor provided, I looked to Google to help me find my heart surgeon. Dr. Ralph Damiano, the head of cardiothoracic surgery at Barnes Hospital stood out among all the others. I trusted his face. I tuned into his essence and grabbed my pendulum for validation that I had found the person best suited to repair my heart. As I researched to learn more about how a calcified valve gets repaired, I felt no fear. I was comforted learning that Barnes

Hospital was one of the best hospitals in the country for heart surgery. I then knew, in that moment, that the reason I was told to move back home was so I could have heart surgery with one of the best surgeons in the United States. Clearly I was on a need-to-know basis with the Holy Spirit. Although the whole picture was not illuminated, each step I needed to take was revealed.

Perhaps all of this was the most grace-filled way to have me make the decisions that had led to me into the office of Dr. Ralph Damiano. When he shared that I needed open heart surgery as quickly as he could get it scheduled, I kidded, "Could we do it tomorrow?" He smiled, empathetically, recognizing the enormity of what I was processing. He looked at me with vast moral authority. His presence was commanding and seemed fearless.

"Regan, I can fix this."

I believed him.

Now my heart was with my children, sensing what this would mean for them. I knew they would be frightened, so I asked in prayer for their guardian angels and guides to work overtime to help comfort what I knew would be heightened emotion and fear in them. I also knew that telling them was going to be the hardest conversation I would ever have. My hope was that my sincere lack of fear would comfort them. I had no fear of death. Over their lifetime, I had expressed to them why. The relevance of my spiritual practice, my awakening, my early schooling was in sharp focus. No better time than facing death to choose to feel fully alive, divinely guided, with a surrendered trust in God's will. When I told them what I had learned from my surgeon, they seemed somehow at peace. They both said quickly, "Mom, I know you'll be fine." Perhaps they said that as a way of comforting themselves, but whatever lay underneath what they said, their response had a grounded, hopeful sincerity to it.

My surgery was scheduled a few weeks out; I was to report to the cardiac surgery center at 5:00 am on July 29th. The surgeon gave me what looked like marketing materials, a binder full of information about the procedure, what to expect post surgery, and detailed instructions of what I needed to do prior to help insure a successful outcome. I was instructed to clean my skin everyday with antibacterial soap, to practice getting out of a chair without the use of my hands, and to always have fresh linens on the bed before going to sleep. One page stood out to me in the binder: a photo showing all the ports, tubes, and machines that I would be connected to in the ICU after surgery. I shared it with the boys so they wouldn't be shocked when they saw me the first time. I knew they would be shocked regardless, but at least they could get a concrete sense of what to expect. I had a battery of tests and the only one that felt scary to me was the cardiac catheter procedure where they would insert a tube in the artery in my wrist, which would travel to my heart where they would inject dye so they could see every nook and cranny of my heart. Given the enormity of the surgery, including the sawing in half of my sternum to access my heart, they wanted to make sure there was nothing else to fix. Having had so few medical procedures in my life, I feared all the tests; I hated getting my blood drawn; and the idea of a tiny tube entering my heart through my wrist filled me with a bit of dread. I brought earplugs to my catheter procedure; I had no interest in hearing the beeping machines or any utterance from the doctors. I instructed them, "I am going to put these earplugs in to block all noise while I lie here and pray. Should you need to tell me anything, feel free to take the earplugs out." They smiled at me and reassured me. As I lay there, I prayed deeply for what felt like a long, long time.

Then I felt the earplug being pulled out of my ear. "Well, Regan, other than this thing you were born with, your heart is in almost perfect shape!" Deeply relieved, now I was all finished with the pre-operative tests and could focus on preparing myself mentally and spiritually for the surgery.

I prayed nearly every hour in the weeks leading up to surgery. My prayer remained the same as always. I didn't pray for a specific outcome; my prayer focused on manifesting the highest good—whatever that was. I began specifically calling in Jesus for guidance. He had faced death with such love and grace. As he had embodied the love of God, transcending even physical death, I figured he was the person most qualified to help me prepare. I sought out books that described the historical Jesus, I reread the Gospels, including those hidden in a jar in Egypt found in 1945, for the gospels of Thomas and Mary Magdelene always held the deepest resonance for me. I also read books that honored the Divine Feminine. I felt deep gratitude for my spiritual practice and for the understanding I had developed over the years as I navigated how to heal from the significant trauma of my early life. I also recognized that the work I had done prior to moving, the conscious goodbye I had made to my life in California, had helped me find abiding peace within myself. I had done a life review prior to moving. It all fit together, a beautiful and purposeful puzzle.

In the final days before surgery, I realized I wanted to convey my love and gratitude to my surgeon and surgical team, so I shopped for gifts for them. I also wanted to convey to my sons my infinite love for them, while also trying to summarize what I had learned over the course of my life. So I composed two letters, one for my medical team and one for my children.

> Dear Dr. Damiano and Surgical Team,
>
> Words are inadequate to express my gratitude to you all for fixing my heart. I am experiencing profound transformation as I prepare for today. Life now has a renewed, embodied feeling of gratitude and purpose. When you face something like this, you have choices,

always. I choose hope, gratitude, and love. You have a sacred role to play here, and I wanted you to know that I love you in the truest *agape* sense of the word, and I will forever feel thankfulness for your expert care. I am a spiritual teacher, and this experience is bringing transmutation. Thank you for playing your part, for repairing my heart and enabling me to live the rest of my days in service to others. I hope you feel deep appreciation for what you do. You change lives everyday, extending life and providing new opportunities for people to be reborn. You have helped to rebirth me. The days leading up to today have been filled with magic. In my prayer and meditation time, I have extended love and gratitude to you all, and I will continue to do so as I recover and heal. Thank you, thank you, thank you. The iron hearts I am giving to you were made by a local blacksmith here in Washington, Missouri. Like a blacksmith, you too are in the business of alchemy. May these be a reminder of my continued gratitude for you all and serve as a reminder for the transformative, vital work you do everyday.

With great love and gratitude,
Regan Kelly

My beloved sons, Connor and Ian,

I love you both so much, words are truly inadequate to express how I feel. And while I fully expect to recover from surgery, there is a remote chance that I could not, so I wanted to take some time to share with you both my reflections about life, what I've learned, and what I hope you both in time will fully understand. We are eternal. The body dies, but the energy, which is who we truly are, lives on forever. We have chosen to incarnate here on Earth to learn how to love. Not love as a sentimental emotion, but love which is the embodiment of God itself. It is vast, intelligent, creative, kind, forgiving, generous energy that knows that we are all one. You are made of the same energy, compacted in this body to learn how to navigate the complexity of this dimension with love. Be honest. Be true to your own heart. Live life fully. Don't take life for granted. Strive to be whole. Do the work to heal from the trauma that results from living in this dimension filled with people who are not yet awake to their Divine nature. Be generous. Find ways everyday to be of service to something greater than your own perceived needs. Meditate everyday, consciously connecting to the energy of love and gratitude and soak in that energy for at least thirty minutes a day. If you do that, you will heal and your perception of life and of the living will change too. Find softness. Life has a way of creating sharpness within. Melt that sharpness with love and gratitude. Radiate love to the unhealed places within you. If someone triggers you, realize the trigger is yours and is a call to heal. Realize that someone else could experience the very same situation and have a completely different reaction; therefore you must understand your reaction is yours and, if negative, it means there is something within you that needs healing. If you don't like where you are in this life right now, do something different! A small change in your daily choices can begin to help you shift. Visualize the life you want, see it in all its dimensions, connect to how you want to feel and feel it. Give sincere thanks for this future state and let it go. Knowing as you surrender and release it, the universal energies begin to create it and you begin to build the neural circuits to support this new state of being. Seriously, do this everyday! Work hard. Success requires effort and discipline. If you are avoiding doing something that you know is in your best interest, just realize your system prefers what it is used to and clings to the familiar. Bust through this first by visualizing yourself doing what you are avoiding and feel yourself enjoying the results of your new efforts. Make amends. If there are people you have harmed in anyway, own it and find a way to make amends by at least sincerely apologizing to the person you have harmed and ask for forgiveness. If that's not possible, do it in prayer. Speaking of prayer, ask your guides and angels everyday to assist you in living your highest good. Ask for the resources, people, and insights you need to come forth to support you living and embodying your highest good, your highest blueprint. Remember that in your heart is a blueprint to guide your actions in this life. Listen to your heart, do as it directs, and you'll find yourself living out your highest intentions for this incarnation. Do this everyday. Have fun! Do the things you love. Spend time in nature. Travel. Talk to strangers as you travel to learn about their values and how they live. There are many different ways to express life. Intend to find your purpose by delving deep within and asking your higher self why you've come here. Listen to your inner guidance and take actions that align with that inner knowing. Be good to one another. A brother bond can be one of the strongest available to anyone. Don't take each other for granted. Be curious about each other. I witness you both making assumptions about each other. Instead, learn. Create shared understanding of each other by having honest, vulnerable dialogue. Strengthen your love by compassionate, appreciative inquiry. Your differences, when harnessed with love and a sense of purpose, can be a magical energy that supports what you want to accomplish here. Harness the strength of your bond by nurturing it. Know that I love you and will always look out for you, whether I'm here on Earth or in some other dimension. I am so proud of how you both have transcended addiction, and I hope what remains unhealed within you, you choose to take on and love so you can transcend it. And for the moments where I have failed, forgive me. I have strived to be a good, loving mother to you both and know that loving you both has been my greatest joy of my life.

I love you both infinitely,
Mom

The night before my surgery, I asked to eat at an old favorite restaurant of mine where, some thirty years ago, Michael and I would dine just before he asked me to marry him. My life with him had taught me so much—my love for him remained in my heart regardless of the circumstances, and so my choice in restaurant was a way to honor him, us, and the sons we had made. Michael came to say hello as Jim, the boys, and I sat down for dinner. He brought me a bouquet of flowers and had written me an email that I will always treasure; his response to my sharing with him the letters I had written to our sons and my surgical team. I had also asked him to be present for the children and to sit with them while I was in surgery. No matter the heartbreak that our union represented, my love still remained.

> Re,
>
> What you have written for your surgical team and the boys is beautiful and magical. I'm certain the inspiration behind your doing so, and the act of scribing your thoughts, has also worked its magic on you as my reading them has had on me. I share your intuition about the outcome of your surgery and know that this is not the end of your corporeal existence, but rather a new phase in which the metaphor of the healing of your wounded heart is the foundation or scaffold from which you are building anew; something even more powerful and transformative. However, if we are mistaken and should divine intent reclaim your spirit, be at peace knowing that the love you brought into my, Jim's, and our sons' world, and into the lives of the many others whom you have touched throughout your life, will have been more than enough to grant you much joy and contentment as you witness this world and your works upon it from within the firmament.
>
> You have loved me more greatly than anyone else, and that is a gift for which I am eternally grateful.
>
> With great love and deep affection,
> Mike
> See you on the other side of this, whenever that may be.

As I drank a glass of red wine, savoring my meal as if it could be my last, I felt deeply loved, connected, and trusting that whatever happened the following day in surgery would be as God intended. As I closed my eyes that night, I trusted God completely and felt my eternal nature. I didn't sleep soundly. I figured it didn't matter, for in a few hours I would be unconscious, hanging out in higher realms as Dr. Damiano fixed my broken heart.

I brought out the gifts for my surgical team as they prepped me for surgery. Before they put me on the gurney to wheel me in to surgery, I looked at them all intently behind my surgical mask, told them how much I loved and appreciated them, and also said, "If you can't guarantee me that any blood I may need doesn't have the Covid vaccine in it, I don't want it."

Then my surgical nurse, with wide-open eyes, whispered in my ear, "Oh my God, you fucking get it!"

We stared knowingly and lovingly at each other as they wheeled me in.

Chapter 26. **Miracle**

As I opened my eyes in the ICU, I was immediately aware that I expected to be there. I hurt, though. My throat raged from having been on life support during surgery, pain that resulted from the tube they placed in my airways so a ventilator could breathe for me. My body quickly reclaimed itself, and I was taken off the ventilator about twenty-five minutes after the surgery had ended. My chest hurt, but not nearly as badly as I thought it would, given that they sawed my sternum in half to access my heart and it was now fused together with wire. I glanced down to see the tubes draining fluid into plastic containers. To my right were monitors tracking me, and I felt deep gratitude for the miracle of modern surgery. IVs were connected to bags of fluid keeping me hydrated and nourished. My nurses were angels on Earth, treating me with deep compassion as I drifted in and out of consciousness in the hours post surgery.

I do not remember much that first day, other than feeling a loving presence within and deep gratitude for being alive. I felt like I was being given a fresh start. I sensed Michael was right: this surgery was a metaphor for healing a wounded heart and building a new life from its renewal. I slept as my children, husband, and best friend waited patiently for me to become fully conscious. I would learn the next day that Connor stayed in my room late into the night and was finally asked to leave my bedside around 1:00 am. As I slept, he texted me.

> I love you and I'm glad you're resting. I just want you to know how much I love you and how this has put so much in perspective for me. Last night was hard because I didn't know if you were going to be okay or not. I prayed to God and I cried and kept saying 'I love you' and if you were going to make it or not, I knew that you would always be with me, and I would always be with you. I am so happy you are okay. I am so grateful for you and your guidance and strength. The doctor said today it was the worst calcification he had ever seen and that he didn't know how you were still alive. When I saw you today, I cried with happiness because you were alive and breathing on your own. It was hard to see you like that, but I'm glad I got to see you at all you know. I want you to know whether I'm right next to you while you sleep or in the hotel or wherever I am, I'm always with you and I'm filling myself up with all the love and light I can take from God and sending it to you. You're so special and I know you're going to feel so much better and live a long life and do everything you set your mind to. I don't know how I could do it without you, Mom. You're the only person I want to talk to right now and I think about how much fun we have together and all the light you bring into the world. You're a superhuman and I can't wait to see the next stage of you and all you accomplish. You motivate me to be better and hold my head up high in the midst of the storm. I get so much of my strength from you and I'm so happy you're still here with me on this crazy rock spinning through the sky. I can't wait for

you to see all that I do and I want you to know that none of it would be possible without all the love and support you gave me in my life. I wish I could take all the pain you have away and experience it instead so you didn't have to. I love you.

Upon receiving that text, I knew I had lived and mothered well. Connor provided me the best medicine in the ICU: his abiding, vast, unconditional love.

Seeing my sweet husband's face was also medicine. He had been so scared prior to surgery and to see him in the ICU still fearful but deeply relieved comforted me. I knew the weeks leading up to surgery, and the surgery itself, were harder on my loved ones than they was on me. Ian stayed mostly away; seeing me in the ICU was more than he could bear. He stayed nearby in a hotel. I knew how much this ordeal had impacted him. Connor preferred to process his feelings alone. Ian, in contrast, sought connection. Sadly for him, he didn't get what he needed as he felt relief that I was okay, yet fear about my current condition.

The next morning I was cleared from the ICU, which is uncommon so soon after surgery, but thankfully they didn't have a free bed in a step-down unit, so I remained there, happily, since the ICU is where you are given the best, most present care. I was in a lot of pain, but the nurses encouraged me to get out of bed to sit in a nearby chair. Apparently the surgical tubes pressing against my nerves caused the pain. Every slight movement I made created the most excruciating pain I had ever known. I couldn't wait until they could take the tubes out. I kept glancing at the containers of fluid, hoping to see less and less as time went on, knowing that if the drainage ended, they would take them out and I could focus more easily on healing and gaining the strength to walk. The nurses kept emphasizing the importance of moving as quickly as possible to accelerate the healing and restoration that comes from getting out of bed.

My favorite nurse, Sam, two mornings after surgery came into my room with a loving smile and exclaimed, "Spa day!" She then lovingly washed and conditioned my hair as I leaned back into a plastic bin that housed warm water. As she carefully washed me, I felt anointed. Hours later, I was told they would be taking the tubes out as well as pacing wires that connected my heart to some kind of machine to charge my heart with electricity if it failed to function correctly. Seeing wires being pulled out of my chest was surreal; feeling them exit was even stranger. Once the tubes were removed, I felt freedom and little pain. Sitting in a chair or walking to the bathroom with assistance was no longer challenging to do. I was motivated. I was determined to get home as quickly as possible. My mother was with me; I could feel her power and the high energy she embodied. She was charging me with her love and power—so much so I felt a bit manic. This energy felt incredibly strong and hopeful.

The only thing I wished was different was the food. The hospital certainly didn't have a food-is-medicine approach. The food was grotesque and my husband felt a bit like DoorDash, heading into the neighborhood to get me food worthy of eating. He brought me wonderful dinners from a local French brasserie, acai smoothies for breakfast, and simply, gladly, did whatever he could to support me. I reflected on how amazing the human body is; open heart surgery on a Friday morning and, come Monday, I was in a regular room, no longer connected to constant monitoring in the ICU, with the strength to walk the halls without help. My surgeon had told me that I would immediately feel better after surgery, given how calcified my aortic valve had been, and, boy, was he right! The contrast was significant. No "heartburn" as I walked. I marveled at how my intuition didn't sense anything wrong prior to being told that fateful morning to "go to the doctor." I never considered that my heartburn might actually be chest pain.

Come Tuesday, just four days after open heart surgery, I was told I would be going home! I felt such gratitude for my nurses who took such exquisite care of me. As I waited for my discharge to process, I showered. The first shower I'd taken since before surgery. It felt like heaven. The steamy water was enlivening. I realized how much I took for granted. I reflected on the miracle of modern plumbing, how you can simply turn a faucet to find clean, hot water. As I felt the magnitude of the moment through a simple everyday act, I committed to myself to try to sustain how alive I felt, how grateful, how hopeful. I put on my makeup, wanting to leave the hospital looking as beautiful on the outside as I felt on the inside. And then Dr. Damiano, the surgeon who had saved my life, came walking in. His presence felt god-like: powerful, commanding, yet supremely loving. He sat on the end of my bed, gave my leg a playful tap, and his gaze then became a bit more intense.

"Regan, I do not have a clinical explanation for you. I simply do not understand how you were alive prior to surgery." He then explained that typically you have about a half-dollar amount of room for blood to flow through the aortic valve. In my case, it was less than the diameter of a Q-tip stick. He shared that it was the worst, most calcified aortic valve he had ever seen in his forty-year career and how he had to scrape bone off my heart for over an hour. He marveled at how well I was doing.

"Do you believe in Jesus Christ?" I asked him.

And he quickly answered, "Yes, yes, I do."

I then said, "Well, that's the only explanation I've got."

Driving home felt like a miracle. Really. I had no pain. I had nothing but love and gratitude in my heart.

Jim sweetly guided me inside. He had bought a step stool to assist me getting into bed. And while I had practiced doing things without the use of my arms, as a way of protecting my broken sternum, I was challenged by not being able to do everyday tasks. I hugged a plush heart pillow anytime I walked to remind me to do everything with great care—and without using my arms. Nurses came to visit, but after the first week of home health care, they said I no longer needed it. They shared how remarkable my recovery was—I exuded high energy and felt no pain. All my vitals were normal. I required no medicine. I was really beginning to understand what Jesus meant when he said, "With God, all things are possible."

It was summer, and I was eager to walk outside, feel the summer heat, and reconnect with my land. I walked with prayerful intention. Each step, I affirmed my health. Each step, I prayed along the perimeter of my ten forested acres. I felt surrounded by unseen forces. I felt so connected to God, to my mother, and to the guides whose voices had saved my life. How I felt as I walked reminded me of how I felt when I had awakened some thirty years before. I paused to rest as I looked at my expansive lawn, the lush forest, my beautiful home, and the building that was being remodeled to serve as my yoga and "come work on your shit" center. I pulled my phone out of my back pocket to capture the moment. When I quickly looked to see what I had photographed, I was taken aback. A light beam, from sky to lawn, stared back at me in the photo. I thanked the energy that was there and felt deep comfort knowing we are never truly alone.

Chapter 27. Inflamed

A few weeks after surgery, I went back to Barnes Hospital to meet my surgeon for a follow up appointment. He commented on how great I was doing as he checked me for leg swelling and reviewed my EKG and echocardiogram. I shared with him that I had a low-grade fever. He commented that he didn't think it was related to surgery and that maybe I had caught a bug. Relieved, I thanked him again for saving my life and told him I would always pray for his wellbeing. He let me know that the iron heart I had given him as a gift was now hanging behind his desk. We had a very strong bond; we both knew that we had experienced a miracle together.

As the weeks passed, my fever remained. Almost everyday I would leave messages through the patient portal with Dr. Damiano's nurse, who continued to say I was doing great and not to worry about the fever—it wasn't unexpected, given the severity of my surgery. But with each passing day, I felt more and more sick. I was experiencing excruciating pain on the top of my left shoulder. I continued to reach out to my surgeon through his nurse, who continued to say there was nothing to worry about. Yet I was getting sicker, hotter, more consumed by pain. The nurse's responses felt negligent.

One day, out of desperation, I sat and prayed. I called in my guides, my ancestors of the highest intention, and Jesus. "Please help. I sense something is really wrong. I need my surgeon to know what is happening. Thank you, and so it is!"

Literally ten minutes after I prayed, my cell phone rang. A woman explained she was subbing for Dr. Damiano's lead nurse and had read all my messages. "Are you okay?"

I quickly responded that no, I wasn't okay. "Can you please find Dr. Damiano and explain to him what is going on? Look him in the eye and then please call me back before the end of the day and let me know what he says."

Thankfully she did just that. "Dr. Damiano wants you to come to the ER right away to get evaluated."

Relieved that I now had his attention, and angry knowing that his other nurse served as gatekeeper and hadn't told him about my symptoms, I packed a bag. Jim drove me back into the city to the hospital where I had been born and then born again. The ER was intense as they drew my blood to try to determine what was wrong. They assumed infection and began to give me high doses of intravenous antibiotics. After a few hours, they transferred me to a regular room where I awaited results.

No infection. They didn't know what was causing my fever, which had climbed to 103. Now under the care of a cardiologist, I answered his questions as best I could as he tried to uncover the cause of the persistent fever. Now mid-September, I had had a fever for almost two months. Perplexed, my cardiologist then humbly asked me, "What do you think is wrong?"

My eyes filled with tears as I took in his question. "Wow, Dr. Sadhu, no doctor has ever asked me that question before. I think my heart is traumatized from the surgery and is inflamed." He ran tests to see if I had inflammation and, within the hour, I was diagnosed with pericarditis—inflammation of the pericardium—the membrane that holds the heart and serves as its protection. The diagnosis made so much sense to me. Given the brutality of what I had experienced—open-heart surgery in some ways is incredibly primitive—I sensed my heart was deeply afraid. I sensed that my heart felt abandoned by me. I had deliberately traveled to higher realms before surgery began; I had exited while my physical heart was brutalized.

In the months that followed, I engaged in daily prayer and meditation to try to convince my heart that surgery had been designed to save our life, not hurt us. Once diagnosed, they put me on the highest amount of ibuprofen they could safely prescribe, hoping that in a couple of weeks the anti-inflammatory medicine would cure me.

My heart was not convinced. For the next five months, I wondered if I was ever going to truly heal. *How ironic it would be if I died from pericarditis*, I thought. *I had a heart that clinically offered no explanation for how it had supported me living, and I am going to die of heart inflammation?* Somehow, the irony gave me hope. I would have some good days and then spiral back down into feeling so sick, tired, with a fever that remained. I remembering coming back from a morning of errands so wiped out that I looked at Jim and said, "I'm not sure I am going to make it."

One night, the thermometer read 104. The medicine was clearly not making any difference. I was instructed to return to the ER. As I entered the ER, I told the receptionist that I had severe pain on top of my left shoulder, a classic pericarditis symptom, and a high fever. Upon hearing this, they'd put me on a gurney with an IV in my arm in a manner of seconds. I could feel the fear of my emergency room doctors and I knew they thought I was having a heart attack. I quickly yelled out that I had pericarditis and they stopped and collectively took a deep breath. Soon I would be admitted again while they figured out how to treat my heart inflammation that wasn't responding to the anti-inflammatory medicine; in fact my inflammation levels were so high, it was as if I was taking nothing at all.

My cardiologist consulted with an endocrinologist to inform how to treat my severe inflammation. As I finally transitioned from the ER to a regular bed, a doctor that worked for my cardiologist greeted me. It was 2:00 a.m., and he had been patiently waiting for me. The commitment of this team was inspiring. They clearly cared. I was then prescribed 40 mg of prednisone, the synthetic equivalent of cortisol, the stress hormone. An hour after taking my first dose, I felt like I could climb Mt. Everest. I would be on a high dosage of prednisone, along with colchicine, and the hope was that in time the medicine would reduce my inflammation and I would be healed. When I returned home with my new treatment protocol, I was hopeful. The prednisone made me feel a bit like a super human—fearlessness with a huge amount of energy. As my inflammation decreased, the medicine would then have me feel like I was becoming insane, or at least incredibly short tempered. I wondered if this was how mass shooters felt. Fueled by chemicals to do acts of violence. And while I wasn't violent, I could relate. Thankfully, my meditation practice kept me somewhat intact. I at least had the presence not to act on my feelings. But my feelings, fueled by cortisol, felt almost out of my control.

As I rested, for it was important to not exert myself, I scrolled on my phone, making décor decisions for my yoga center. The walls were now built, the new floors installed, fresh paint created a loving vibe, all that was needed were new chandeliers and furnishings to create a welcoming place for my group teaching. I envisioned open space with ample room for at least thirty yoga students and a cozy living room that would inspire the connection and vulnerability needed to do deep work. I saw myself sitting on one of the circular-shaped sofas leading classes for small groups or working one-on-one with people seeking support for their inner life. I looked for furnishings loved by other five-star buyers and quickly purchased what was needed to finish decorating my space. My contractor installed the large chandeliers I had ordered, which made a big difference. It felt loving, welcoming, and elegant. In a few weeks, my center was complete.

Now all that was needed was to convince my heart to come back into balance so I could fully recover. Each day I would talk to my heart, telling it how much I loved and appreciated it. I honored the intense trauma it had endured. Since inflammation is the body trying to protect itself, I thanked my heart for keeping me safe. I felt a bit like I was in the midst of a high-stakes negotiation, trying to convince my heart that it was now safe to put its guard down and fully live.

As fall turned to winter, I began to feel better. My endocrinologist, who now was leading my treatment, counseled me to begin tapering down my medicine, taking a bit less with each passing week. Every Friday I would drive to the lab to get my blood drawn to determine my inflammation levels. I was encouraged that as I took less and less medicine, my inflammation continued to decrease. I kept vigilant with my prayers and continued to convince my heart that it was now safe to surrender, to fully process what had occurred, to honor the trauma and my heart's point of view of needing to protect me via inflammation. I thanked my heart throughout each day for being courageous and committed to my protection, while also trying to persuade it that it was no longer necessary to stand guard. Now late December, I greeted the coming winter solstice with deliberate reverence. I reflected on how I had learned to embrace my darkness and to transmute fear by fully connecting to the power of Divine love.

On winter solstice itself, I intuitively knew I was finally healed. I had spent the last five months mostly in bed, allowing my heart to find its way to renewal. I saw how all of my darkest moments served me by teaching me how to transmute them through love.

As I drove to the lab for my weekly blood draw, having tapered my medicine down to taking none at all for a week, I knew that my results would declare that my inflammation was finally gone. And indeed, upon receipt of my results later that day, as darkness set in for the longest night of the year, I was healed.

Chapter 28. In Service

I was healed, but, after five months in bed, my muscles had atrophied. I began to exercise again, heading to our local Y to use the weight machines. I also began doing yoga everyday. I found a wonderful studio in Wildwood, about thirty miles from my home, and began going to classes. While I knew yoga, I found motivation practicing with others in a studio setting. I was getting stronger with each passing day and was eager to open my own center and begin sharing what I knew to be true: we are made of energy and each of us is a unique expression of the Divine. I wanted to share my intimate journey of how I faced a life-threatening illness, how I had cultivated a deep commitment to prayer, and how the voices of my guides led me to Washington, Missouri, first so I could heal and then so I could serve. I wanted to be a beacon of hope given all the trauma I had known, yet I had found a way through accessing and embodying Divine love to transmute it into meaning, purpose, self-acceptance, and forgiveness.

The daughter of the former owner of my home became a valuable assistant. She created a Facebook presence for my center and helped me with the details needed to begin getting the word out in my community about who I was and what I offered. Heeding my inner guidance, I began offering yoga as an act of service at no charge. I didn't want there to be an economic barrier to learning yoga, and I hoped that in practicing with me, people would become more curious about improving their inner health. With the help of a local firm, I began promoting my center. Word was getting out that I had something profound to offer. In just a few months, hundreds of people would come and practice with me. I began working with private clients, helping them process their traumas while learning how to access the intelligence of the heart. I facilitated an offsite for a corporate team. I was creating momentum and it all felt like God's doing. I felt purposeful, grateful, and fully alive.

In late March I learned that a dear friend—the former minister at the Unity Church that had housed my grade school, where I had led a youth group, and who had given me the social support I needed post-awakening as my Jedi training to teach me how to love darkness—had died. He had developed blood clots after back surgery, fell into a coma, and never came back. The Covid vaccine was killing so many and a common deathly side effect was blood clots. Shocked at the news, I immediately made plans to fly to Florida for his memorial to honor his memory. I appreciated deeply that his service would be held on Palm Sunday, the day that marks the first day of Holy Week, as we reflect on Jesus' courageous entry into Jerusalem. As Jesus entered the Holy city, crowds had gathered quoting Psalm 118:25–26 which had prophesized the coming of the Messiah. I felt that Lawrence was grateful that we would gather to honor him on that Holy Day. I had hoped I would see others that I knew at his funeral, yet I was the only one from the St. Louis church who had made the trip. Lawrence was a Christian mystic who had taught me so much as I navigated the polarity of my post-awakening experience. I couldn't believe that he was dead. As I cried in the service, I thought of my mother who had always commented that I never seemed to have a tissue when I needed one. Tears rolled down my cheeks, my nose becoming clogged with emotion, as I reflected on the magic that was Lawrence.

After the service, I returned to my hotel, eager to put on my bathing suit and head to the beach. Jim had sweetly bought me a new suit that had a zipper in the front so I could zip it up to protect my surgery scar from the sun. Something about grieving Lawrence had me recounting and reviewing my life yet again. I had lived so much life since knowing Lawrence at twenty-seven. I sensed he was proud of me, holding me in deep love with a pinch of awe for all that I had known and experienced. I undressed and headed to the bathroom naked to brush my hair and put on sunblock. As I stared at myself in the mirror, I was taken aback by what I saw. It looked as if my scar had changed. The blue lotus oil that I had used everyday to help it heal had done an extraordinary job, for the scar was faint. But as I got closer to the mirror, I truly couldn't believe my eyes. A faint cross on my chest, the symbol of the sacrifice Jesus had made, stared back at me. My scar was now in the shape of a crucifix.

A few months later, I returned to the hospital for my one-year check-up post surgery. Enlivened by the work I was doing at my center, awed by the miracle of it all and how the miracle of what I endured was now reflected in my flesh, I felt vibrant and healthy. Given that it was Tuesday and I knew that was the only day my surgeon was in the office, I hoped I could see him after my appointment with my cardiologist. After an EKG and a brief visit affirmed my health, I asked my doctor, "Is Dr. Damiano here today? I have something I need to show him." Indeed he was there and, serendipitously, he was in a room just across the hall from where I was. The room felt serious—doctors staring at screens at their workstations, typing with intention what I assumed was their charting for the surgeries they had performed. I peeked my head into the room with a huge smile on my face. "Dr. Damiano? It's Regan." He looked so handsome, for I had never seen his face without a mask. He jumped up out of his chair with such delight on his face.

"You look incredible!" he exclaimed. The other doctors glanced away from their monitors for a moment to see who had interrupted their work.

"Remember when we visited on my day of discharge and you explained that you had no clinical explanation for me? And I responded by asking you if you believed in Jesus?"

"Of course I do, how could I forget any of it," he replied.

"Well, I have something I need to show you." I then pulled down my blouse to reveal my scar. As he took it in, tears began rolling down his angular cheeks. The other doctors sensed something and stood up, now encircling me as they stared at my chest.

Dr. Damiano, overcome with feeling, looked at his team and asked them, "Have you ever seen anything like this?" They all shook their heads *no* as their eyes filled up with tears. Then Dr. Damiano hugged me with such devotion, looked at me deeply, and said, "Well, Regan, that's another miracle because there wasn't any horizontal cutting. Could you please send me a picture of it?"

I assured him I would as I walked out of the room. My heart was wide open as I felt into the miracle of it all. I then knew how my book would end.

And so it has.

Epilogue

I continue to be of service in Washington, Missouri, through my yoga and "come work on your shit" center. I named my center Aset, after the goddess of love, the true Egyptian name of the goddess whom we know as Isis, for that is what the Greeks called her. I teach yoga twice a week as an act of service at no charge, just as I had been directed. I share what I know about healing trauma and how to connect to higher intelligence, which I call Inner Life Coaching. I am committed to loving my clients as fully as I can so they can learn to love themselves. Every few months I teach HeartMath to small groups. I host corporate offsites and help teams navigate uncertainty, ambiguity, and stress—the norms of today's workplace. I have hosted four plant medicine ceremonies facilitated by shamanic practitioners I trust. I will be teaching my Ready to Awaken curriculum come fall. I continue to pray and meditate as a daily practice.

When I enter my center each day, walking the short distance from the main house, I burn Palo Santo, walk the perimeter of the 2,800 square feet space, as I pray, "Sweet loving spirit, angels of love and light, my guides, my beloved Yeshua and Mary Magdalene, my guardians, ancestors of the highest vibration and intention, I ask for you to be with me. Bring me the insights, the resources and the people to live my highest good, my highest blueprint for this incarnation. I ask that the souls that I am best equipped to support come through my door. Thank you. I love and appreciate your support so much. You are invaluable to me."

While I have been open just over a year, more than two hundred fifty people have come to my yoga classes, and I am beginning to build a presence on social media to bring my message of love, faith, resilience and discipline to the world. As I approach my 58th birthday, I have nothing but gratitude for the privilege of aging.

My family is well. Ian is a personal trainer at our local Y, continuing to earn straight A's in his college coursework. He has made some great friends with like-minded men in our small town, and is thriving. My husband is now semi-retired and finds ways everyday to support me in doing as God directs. He has reversed his diabetes, lost at least thirty more pounds, and gets his steps in everyday. Connor remains sober and is building a life in San Jose with a wonderful woman who has been committed to him since before he entered rehab. Michael leaves for Africa in a few weeks, directed by God to be of service there. He has built a trusted, loving relationship with his sons and continues to be disciplined in his spiritual life. He remains one of the few people I can talk about current events and the power of Jesus' love. Our love will always be bigger than the circumstances we created together. My cat loves hunting rodents on our estate, though spends most of his time indoors. I have made deeply resonant friendships in my new town and Sara, the owner of the Blu Room, has become my dearest friend and collaborator. Life now is as I always dreamed it could be.

What I hope you take away from my story is hope. My aim was to inspire you to begin the courageous journey to heal—from your childhood trauma, from ancestral trauma—by making different choices than your ancestors did and offering them your sincere forgiveness and unconditional love. I want you to know that you are not alone. You are surrounded by an intelligence that loves you and will help you, but you must ask. Like the "prime directive" in

Star Trek, your guides and angels won't interfere unless you explicitly ask for their help. So ask. Learn how to create quiet within so you can hear and heed the call of your unseen support while creating the inner conditions that provide ease, flow, and the felt connected sense of your divinity. Harness the energy of love, not to bypass your pain, rather as your trusted companion to travel deep within to all the scary, dark, traumatized places within you, for it all needs your love and acceptance. Embrace the cyclical nature of life. Healing is a process, and conscious Divine embodiment requires discipline. We never reach a "final" destination in our understanding of God or ourselves. Rather, we ebb and flow, sometimes losing our way. There are no mistakes, only lessons. Learn to forgive and to see how the complexity of life with Divine perspective makes perfect sense. It was all necessary to bring you to this moment. And know, just as Jesus said, "With God, anything is possible."

Acknowledgments

This sharing of my story was made possible by the unconditionally loving support of my beloved husband Jim Kelly. His commitment to me, his capacity to ride this wave of life with a steady, consistent heart provided me the freedom to heal and the freedom to express the fullness of what I have learned to be of service of others. Words are inadequate to express the depth of my love.

To my sons, who inspire me everyday to show up for them with fierce, unwavering love. You both embody the Divine masculine and I am immensely proud of you both!

To my editors Brad Wetzler and Lauren Larsen, your expert care, enthusiastic support and belief in me kept me going. To Lisa Hermann, who appeared in my life at just the right time, offering me her beautiful design mind and marketing genius to help shepherd my message to the world. You have become an invaluable part of my team and a trusted friend. Thank you.

And to my readers, KEEP GOING!

Visit regancaruthers.com for more inspiration, tools and support and if on Instagram let's connect @ReganCaruthers.

Printed in the USA
CPSIA information can be obtained
at www.ICGtesting.com
LVHW020435081124
795973LV00003B/442